THE RACE

THE RACE

What's wrong with capitalism and how to fix it

LUTHER S. WISSA

Created with Vellum

Contents

This book is dedicated to Safwat and Eshraka Wissa, my parents, without whom's challenge and encouragement this book would never have been possible. Also, to Fady Wissa who bore the brunt of house work as I was locked away writing for 10–12 hours a day and Weam Salam who helped me escape my self-imposed isolation. And finally, I dedicate this book to those who lost their voice, as a shout to those who lost their hearing.

Foreword

Some men see things as they are and ask why. I dream of things that never were, and ask why not.

JFK

Looking back, I vividly remember telling my first-grade classmates at the School for the Protection of Eye Sight in Cairo, Egypt: "soon, I'm going to America." At that time, I equated going to the United States to winning the lottery. I also viewed it as evidence of my superiority over my peers who were to remain in Egypt.

I continued to declare my impending superiority for eight years. Finally, in 1997, my family and I moved to the land of the free and the home of the brave. Where, dare I say, I have done well for myself, through hard work and constant self-examination and correction.

However, this book is not wholly concerned with my journey. Rather, it is about our story, not only the story of where we were, but where the human race is going. A story about this rat race that we all call life.

The purpose of this book is to introduce a few new ideas. Some of these ideas I learned after finishing the book that they were not all entirely new. However, the main point of what I plan to introduce is new. When I first embarked on this line of thinking, I had no desire to write anything, not so much as an article, let alone a book. If at the end of 2019 I was asked to list 100 goals I wished to accomplish in life, "write a book" would not have made the list.

Out of moral necessity, I came to feel that I must write this book. The reason? For observing injustice and not speaking out against it, is itself an act of injustice.

Since I started writing this book, the world has changed drastically and rapidly than anyone could have thought possible. These changes happened in only four months. As I add this in August 2020, it seems we are living in a new world from the April 2020 world, a much more dangerous world to the one we thought we would have by now. I shudder to think what the next four months might bring.

Introduction

All new lofty ideals and aspirations may at first seem dangerous (or even repugnant), but I promise that if you stick with me, in the end, you will see the world differently, and maybe even agree the new way forward is the only way out.

I know many people want to improve how most of the world is living, but do not have a concrete solution. Of late, the dream of globalization is anathema to many. I cannot blame any of its critics; instead, I intend to add my voice to theirs. The architects of such a dream, namely the instigators of globalization, are turning out to be only slightly better than the architects of the USSR. I suspect we will end at a much worse place before they are done building their dream and our nightmare. Now we reached a point that we are facing our failure at every side, not only in America, but also worldwide. As the global nightmare grows, the world inches closer to another large-scale conflict, unsurprisingly since conflict has been the perpetual mode of human existence.

I plan to introduce an idea that lowers the inherent desire in humans to fight. After reading this book, Americans will face an exceedingly demanding decision. This decision will not require great intellect, but what will be needed is strength of character; every moral leap forward that we have made in human history has always mandated character long before intelligence. First, we must decide the morally correct way to live, and then we must choose how to restructure our world to align to our stated values.

Intentions and results are not the same. With their supposed kindness, the elite of America have helped some in other countries rise to the detriment of the poor and middle class here, while always enriching themselves. In the name of rationalism and globalization, the American elite have thrown the American workers to the jackals of global competition and neoliberal capitalism. In response, America has lost all those elements of its culture that made it unique. Consequently, the American worker will throw America into the arms of any semi-dictator, presuming that anything is better than what they have now. Trump will not be the last semi-dictator leading America. Instead, he is the first of many strong men in Stalin or Hitler's mold that we are destined for, all as a result of despair. The whole world is moving toward authoritarianism once again. As the American elite abandons America for globalization, the American workers will abandon America for isolationism. Fool me for 50 years, shame on you, fool me for another 50 years, shame on me.

The most challenging life choices are often not difficult to understand, but they are enormously difficult to implement. The second hardest sentence that relates to morality is "don't harm yourself or another." Any child can understand this sentence, yet an incredible number of books have been written to teach us how to live by this ideal. When it comes to achieving such a simple command, we are as far as the east is from the west in reaching that standard. Again, we all now understand that a king installing his son as a king in his place is wrong; as a matter of fact, the Germans understood it right after Rev. Martin Luther translated the Bible from Latin to German in the 1500s. German peasants fought a war with the aristocracy over the oppression of the nobility, the aristocracy won that war, that victory limited human progress for centuries.

Two hundred and fifty years later, another war in America occurred which convinced the United Kingdom that feudalism needed to stop. Fortunately, this time the aristocracy lost. The hindrance was not in the moral idea, the obstacle is always found in our willingness to implement and enforce its consequences. Again, when it came to slavery, we now accept that having another human being as property is inexcusable. Yet, in the United States we needed a civil war to convince the south to stop that which we all now agree is reprehensible. After reading this book, Americans will face a new reprehensible idea that is easy to understand, yet exceedingly difficult to live and implement.

My sincere desire is that no one will resort to any form of violence after reading this book. In the past violence may have been necessary but now we have free-speech and democracy those are now the correct mechanisms to bring change. Actual change only occurs when we revolutionize and elevate our morality and ethics then based on new ethics we can create new economics. Even after the north won the civil war it took decades if not a century to create a slaveless economics in the south, not to mention a change in attitude. We are still struggling with equality of opportunity. To improve people's lives, we don't need better math or better technology, rather we need a better understanding of our reality and, most crucially, a better understanding of ourselves. Before we look into how we improve America, it's imperative to ask: why do we need change?

Many books have been written arguing for change. Three books I would recommend which offer a good summary of the two sides are, *The System* by Robert Reich, *Spirit Level* by Richard Wilkson and Kate Pickett, and *Coming Apart* by Charles Murray. Two of these books are concerned with the United States. However, it's all of humanity that is in trouble. The United States holds the keys of the global economy. They have pushed the whole world into becoming extremely capitalistic. As a result, other countries are forced to become more capitalistic, consciously overlooking all its adverse effects. There is a slew of books from both the right and left that identify enormous challenges facing the United States today. In most cases, these books agree on many of the "problems," even if they differ in their solutions. The fact that both sides identify some of the same concerns is very telling. If your truly brave and will medicated you can read *Suicide of a Superpower* by Patrick Buchanan, *America: the Farewell Tour* by Chris Hedges, or *The Myth of Capitalism* by Denise Hearn and Jonathan Tepper, all of which I found after writing the book all these cemented my original view.

However, long before I read any of these books, I started reflecting on why humanity is in such a mess. Any new knowledge has always begun with the desire to question the current state of affairs. From "Why did the apple fall on my head?" to "Why are we in such a mess?" Some US citizens might not see any reason to change. However, if they are honest with themselves, they will realize that the current systems have created vast inequality and have benefited them more than others around the world. This may be because they reside in the top 10% of the world's wealthiest countries (or they are a top earner in a developing country and that way things appear fine in their eyes).

The situation globally and domestically is far from good or even tolerable. If people need more convincing, I wholeheartedly encourage them to read the books mentioned above. I can sympathize with the lack of insight, I, too, was once blissfully ignorant. That is, until I made a personal discovery and learned about the world. This realisation partly came when I lost $300,000 on the stock market (shhh, don't tell my mom). As long as a person is well off, it's rare that they look back and see how life is for others. Rarely do we recognize whom we have harmed to get at the front of the pack. Some might say to me: "the fact that you are an immigrant who had $300,000 to lose proves the system is working." I will answer that question later in this book. Once I noticed the actual state of America, and our world, I realized we must change. This neoliberal capitalism is entirely illogical, immoral, and, what's more, destructive to our mental health, not to mention that it creates awful economic imbalance. With one change, we can do it all much better. We need a change because if we screw up again, next time we might not get another chance to behave correctly. Often it takes a war to teach us how to treat each other better. We learned a painful lesson during World War I and World War II, nationally and internationally, yet many have already forgotten that lesson. Instead of stealing from other countries the decision was made to shift the theft more internally with each country expanding the wealth gap to unimaginable levels in its borders all in the name of neoliberal capitalism. Will we discover a better way to treat each other or is another painful lesson in order?

Before I began this book, I was asked, "Who are you writing to in this book?" I found this question difficult to answer and even a strange line of thinking. That question implies it's impossible to write a book for everyone. There are three ways in which this would be argued to be true. Firstly, providing arguments to convince a Christian and the arguments to convince a secular can't be the same. Secondly, the words that convince the rich and the words that convince the poor can't be the same. Lastly, and the trickiest of all, the arguments that persuade a Republican and the ideas that convince a Democrat are mutually exclusive. However, I disagree. I believe that the overwhelming majority of people are the same; we are moral and logical creatures. Therefore, like the apostle Paul before me, I intend to be all things to all men.

I will sometimes speak with an Atheist tongue, at other times, use the Christian tongue, sometimes with the tongue of the Republican, and at other times with the tongue of a Democrat. If you find this difficult, I apologize. It's not my intention to offend you. My intention is only to convince you of a better way.

if you feel I'm with you I ask you to please hold your enthusiasm. For in the course of reading the rest of the book, I'm likely to unintentionally offend you, stating an opinion that you disagree with. If you feel I am against you, I assure you I am not. I understand how others' views can feel like a personal assault. However, I will not self-censor lest someone gets offended. The truth is more important than anyone's feelings (mine included).

For though I be free from all men, yet have I made myself servant unto all, that I might gain the more.

And unto the Jews, I became as a Jew, that I might gain the Jews; to them that are under the law, as under the law, that I might gain them that are under the law; To them that are without law, as without law, (being not without law to God, but under the law to Christ,) that I might gain them that are without law.

To the weak became I as weak, that I might gain the weak: I am made all things to all men, that I might, by all means, save some.

1 Cor 9:19-22(KJV)

ONE

Fate or Consequence

Once we hear of a plane crash, we are more preoccupied with the risk of such an event happening to us for a while thereafter, when in reality a car crash is far more likely. Only a few people ever worry about disasters that have never happened before. In response those few who sound the alarm are often ignored or silenced, since the majority are preoccupied with money or the lack thereof. Three years before hurricane Katrina hit, "The Times-Picayune," had devoted several days of coverage to a special series, *Washing Away*. In the series, reporters claimed that officials were "tempting fate" by failing to address weaknesses in the levees meant to protect New Orleans, and cautioned that it was "only a matter of time before South Louisiana takes a direct hit from a major hurricane." (Adrienne LaFrance).

This kind of obliviousness to impending disaster is pervasive and repeated often. Five years or so ago, President Barack Obama and Bill Gates warned us of a possible pandemic, Yet, some in the media and the Trump administration refused to heed this warning, and the consequences of that willful blindness will be with us for decades to come.

The aim of this book is to point out the impending end of our American experiment at the hands of neoliberal capitalism and, more importantly, to shine a light on a new path forward. Many are oblivious to the impending disaster which is poised to surpass all others. Instead they are choosing to be ignorant, some just pray about it, others are stockpiling food and weapons for when "the shit hits the fan." Such actions are understandable in this environment but are insufficient. Yet instead of being reactive can we be proactive and decide to change course? Can we be humble enough to admit no matter how big our ship is, the ice could be bigger? It's time to divert this Titanic before another unthinkable happens. After reading this book you will either do what we humans are accustomed to doing and ignore the warning, or you will heed this warning and do something before it's too late. It's my hope you choose to deal with it before reality teaches us how small we really are.

As a country and as a world, I see us destroying ourselves and our planet's ecology. This will be either at the hands of World War III, through global warming or by yet unforeseen means. Make no mistake, our pseudo-logic is what got us to this point. The United States will not get out of this impossible position and genuinely move forward as a country unless we make some monumental shifts in our collective understanding of reality.

Taxing the wealthy is not a new idea. Giving the wealthy more tax breaks is an even older idea. Building bigger and better weapons to keep others in check is not new. We must see the world differently before we can comprehend the way to fix it. We must stand outside of the "structure" to see what's the matter with the foundations.

The biggest obstacle to improving the system is us, we humans are in it and contrary to popular opinion, we are not "homo economicus." We are much more complicated than that. We are beings who can be full of greed, who use pseudo-logic to deceive ourselves and others into imagining we are angels when we are so often the opposite. Seldomly we are better than we believe ourselves to be, but frequently we are much worse than we are willing to admit, especially to ourselves. That is where religion comes in. Judaism taught us "an eye for an eye." Then Jesus taught us "love your neighbor as yourself," giving us the hardest commandment in history. To advance in science, engineering, or technology and, more to the point to help a hurting world, our morality has to advance significantly. Our ethics must outpace our technology if we hope to survive. It is impossible to progress by cheating and stealing from other countries, as China does, and still hope to lead the world. Also, we in the United States cannot advance by bombing countries on a whim, forcing change in other countries, and acting like the world's bully. The US's moral standing has been deteriorating internationally since World War II as a result of such actions.

America needs to lead not by using powerful weapons

and armies, but by creating "a more perfect union" leading by example. That is what we have aimed to do for hundreds of years. We can't take a system our citizens have come to despise and hope to export it to the rest of the world. In 1792 the French did not overthrow their monarchy because the CIA instituted a regime change in that country, they instigated change because they observed that the American system was better than theirs and that American citizens were better off than French citizens. For a long time now, America has been shifting from the world's role model of freedom and equality to the world's promoter of inequality in the guise of forced happiness. In essence, the job of the United States has been to tell the world "do as I say not as I do."

When the United States was attacked on 9/11 and thousands of innocent lives were lost, where were our Christian ideals in Jesus's words of "love your enemy" or even the universal law of "an eye for an eye."? Rather than rising to those ideals, we reacted with rage and wounded pride. The United States once more reverted to its tendency to over-punish and in retaliation for 9/11, we responded by spreading more havoc, death, and destruction many times more devastating than anything done to us. Consequently, we have paid a tremendous price for this. It cost us tens of thousands of lives and trillions of dollars to wage those wars, and again, we needed to learn, sowing destruction only reaps us harm. Being the world's police is hard work. This task the American people did not ask for. It was born out of World War II and our responsibility to a chaotic world. We had to meet the challenge of keeping the peace and just as we need to help our peacekeepers in the United States do better, we as the world's peacekeepers need to do better.

We should not be astonished at these behaviors; they reflect human nature. The problem is truly exasperated when we begin to promote the worst parts of ourselves. If we form a society with the ideal that "hate is good," what effect does that have on society? How would the term "hate is good" affect how citizens treat each other? In no time, our citizenry would fight and kill each other on the streets, as easy as they drink water, and then we would be required to create laws prohibiting fighting and killing. When a man murders his fellow countryman, a judge would say "killing is against the law." Unfortunately, the reply would inevitably be, "but your honor I was taught that 'hate is good' and if hate is good and because of my hate I have become a murderer, then you taught me to be a murderer as well as to hate." Fixing actions is a fool's errand if we continue to ignore ideals. When we place society's goals behind us (as the book *The End of History and the Last Man* did), we slowly will move backward, only if societies goals are ahead of us will we improve not degenerate.

Let's take another example: in the United States, we want people to work hard, but we glorify laziness every day. So, this time we say "laziness is good," not in words but actions. One can't say laziness is good with actions and "work hard" with words, actions *will always* speak louder than words to the next generation. We know the value of hard work, yet we only advertise people who are partying and dancing and vacationing (in a sense being lazy) and then wonder, why doesn't America's next generation want to work hard? Why don't they value hard work as past generations have? Is it because we told them, through our actions, not to appreciate hard work but to anticipate retirement? We know that work is satisfying and fulfilling, so why does every rich parent say "I worked hard to get where I am so that my kids don't have too"? Why not? Working hard is great, it's useful and much more fulfilling than continuous partying. Hedonism has only one outcome: despair. For we despair of pleasure just as we despair of suffering.

The best behavior we can exhibit by example to the next generation is a good work ethic. That is more fulfilling than fancy cars or trips around the world. It's better than a meaningless existence in the pursuit of pleasure. If we know this, we don't live it. A purpose in life is truly what every soul yearns for, maybe that's why the book "purpose driven life" sold 12 million copies worldwide. Yet now most can't find meaning since they are too busy searching for an extra dollar. The best predictor of future success was hard work, not intelligence; now it's sadly neither. Seven out of ten low IQ individuals who are born to wealthy parents achieve financial Independence by the age of 25. Praising a child's intelligence has proven to be a bad strategy in raising successful children. It's also proven that praising children for their hard work is the best way to help them succeed and find fulfillment.

Considerable social science research has found that constant praise of children can backfire, because it so often consists of telling children how smart they are, not of praising children for the things they do. As a result, many children become protective of their image of being smart and are reluctant to take chances that might damage that image.

Charles Murray, *Coming Apart: The State of White America, 1960–2010*

If you wish your children success, don't tell them "you're very smart" rather tell them "you are such a hard worker." Intelligence is perceived as outside our control, but hard work anyone can do.

I spent many years unlearning the harmful lessons I was taught, some of which I held dear, a portion of which I was taught as a child growing up in Egypt. While most of what I know now I learned as a young man growing up in America. We all have been indoctrinated either by family or by the elite in Hollywood or academia. Sadly, most don't question these lessons and in time we identify with these self-destructive ideas accepting them as a part of our identity.

Consequently, once accepted we refuse to question the old lessons. For in questioning the indoctrination we feel that we are attacking ourselves. In the West, we often hate family indoctrination, but love Hollywood's and academia's indoctrination. As for the east, it's often the family or the state and not Hollywood that is the main indoctrinator. We must recognize that our indoctrination is not who we are. I was fortunate (or perhaps especially cursed) to have been indoctrinated by each side consecutively, once by family and the other by society. The ability to change your mind does not diminish your worth or invalidate your past, instead it's the only mechanism of growth in your life. That being said, we must allow the best words and ideas to shape us. If new words and opinions are not allowed to shape us in a vain attempt at what some view as self-assertion, all we succeed in doing is permit old words and opinions to keep us from improving. Rejecting both forms of indoctrinations is what prompted this book. I found myself in a camp of one. I will endeavor to free the next generation from this cruel master we call capitalism while not losing myself to the hideous post-truth, morally relative cult.

Facing the fear of self-examination is the first challenge, for without self-examination, how can we know where we need to improve? The last fear we need to face is fear of the unknown. Without taking a step into the unknown, nothing new will ever happen.

> *People are usually afraid of change because they fear the unknown. But the single greatest constant of history is that everything changes.*
>
> Yuval Noah Harari, *Homo Deus: A History of Tomorrow* (2017)

Without correctly identifying what got us to this point in human development, our aimless desire for change will create only harmful change. Without correctly acknowledging our history, we are doomed to repeat its mistakes.

Slowly and with much assistance I faced my fear of self-examination and recognized a lesson that we were all taught and we all must unlearn.

One lesson that I was not taught as a child but learned after immigrating to the United States, was "greed is good." The lesson stated "we all must do whatever it takes to get ahead." I remember sitting in a history class in 1999, fresh off the boat, and hearing a summary of Adam Smith's original words, "It is not from the benevolence of the butcher, the brewer, or the baker that we expect our dinner, but from their regard to their interest. We address ourselves, not to their humanity but their self-love, and never talk to them of our necessities but of their advantages." Loosely interpreted by most as "greed is good," or the way it was written in my social studies book, "do the best for you and it will be the best for everyone." From the day I heard that sentence, I knew it didn't make any sense. Even as a child I would envision hundreds of scenarios in which that sentiment proved wrong. But hearing that sentence marked my introduction to indoctrination and pseudo-logic. However, being a child, I hardly thought of it again.

Looking back now, I know that such a lesson was wrong and the only reason such pseudo-logic worked was because American culture was firmly rooted in Christian ideology. Without which, the "best for me" philosophy would lead people to cheat and steal and oppress at every turn, which is precisely what China is doing. Only instead of one person doing that, the CCP (Chinese Communist Party) is trying to leverage 1.4 billion people to do what's best for a few power elites. We, here in the United States, are not much better. Some are leaving the hard work to 350 million only for a few to reach hereto unimagined heights of wealth and cruelty.

In fact, we should say "do what's best for others and it will be what's best for you." Neither is entirely accurate. Yet starting with others is actually closer to reality. Starting with others is what we try to do, it's what actually sparks our creativity. We think to ourselves, "how can I make my life or others' lives better?" With such thinking we innovate, hence constructing a better world for all. As G. K. Chesterton said in "orthodoxy" "They are universal only in the sense that they take one thin explanation and carry it very far. But a pattern can stretch for ever and still be a small pattern. They see a chessboard white on black, and if the universe is paved with it, it is still white on black. Like the lunatic, they cannot alter their standpoint; they cannot make a mental effort and suddenly see it black on white." Our world is full of such lunatics throughout history proclaiming "do the best for you and it will be the best for others" never imagining to turn the sentence around. The consequences of turning that sentence around is the point of this book. People tended to strive for one of three goals: create something first before anyone else, create something better than what previously existed, or create something cheaper than what once existed. All three are examples of doing what's best for others, not what's best for the self. Doing what's best for others is what is useful, it is what's needed. If we use Adam Smith's butcher as an example, he sold tasty meat, sold cheaper meat, or made sure he was closest to his customers. When you teach people to start with themselves and act selfishly, you end up with a broken society. You end up with a $25 trillion debt because you created a system in which the poor cheat to get what they need, the middle cheat to keep what little they have, and the rich cheat to pay no taxes. Teaching "greed is good" is akin to telling citizens to ask not what I can do for my country, ask what my country can do for me. Many years after I first heard Adam Smith's well-known sentence, I learned that Professor Nash (from the movie *A Beautiful Mind*) argued against that same selfishness. Only by then I had absorbed all the wrong lessons and the indoctrination was complete. I had already learned to do what's best for me regardless of the consequences to others.

In 2013, as a top salesman at Verizon, I had a keen eye for working out how to cheat the system to meet my quota (in other words, do what's best for me), as each store, and consequently each salesperson, had a quota. We had to surpass the previous year's numbers to get paid a higher amount of money each year. The higher above the base quota we sold, the more money we made also if you fall behind the quota you get much less if anything. The previous year we knew the salespeople in our store worked extremely hard to meet their quota since half the salesforce is still present from the previous year. Year after year the requirements increased. As a salesforce, we were losing the battle. Fewer and fewer representatives reached their goals, and most of the high achievers were achieving success by some form of cheating. They were cheating fellow employees, cheating the customer, or cheating the company. I'm not saying all salespeople are immoral. Instead, I did whatever I had to do to meet my quota. Both the Wells Fargo and AT&T scandals are recent examples of the outcome of this overwhelming pressure to perform and its destructive results.

I knew how to cheat (manipulate) the customer to meet my quota. So, when it was to my advantage, I cheated Verizon for the customer's sake (without breaking any rules). However, only when it helped me meet my quota would I cheat for the customer. I was the top salesperson in two key metrics above thousands of other salespeople in Verizon's best sales region across the United States. As a consequence of my high achievement, I was promoted and subsequently fired for something trivial, which was only a perceived injustice and in truth was the least of my "crimes." The problem with society today is that I am not alone, most of us who do any kind of "climbing of the corporate ladder" or high financial achievement have indulged in some form of cheating. Capitalism started as useful human endeavors do, with the best of intentions. It began by rewarding the most efficient and now it's ending by awarding the cruellest. It's human nature to try and improve our status; we will do all we can to get ahead. When it helps us and helps others, then that is great. But often when it helps us and harms others, we are just fine with that as well, better yet we convince ourselves "no one is getting harmed."

The fault, dear Brutus, is not in our stars, but in ourselves, that we are underlings.

Julius Caesar (I, ii, 140-141)

I would venture to guess that if Shakespeare lived in modern times the line would go something like: "The fault, dear Brutus, is not in our algorithms, but in ourselves." Alternatively, he might write: "The problem is not in our technology but in our greed." We justify our most harmful actions to ourselves. The thinking goes: "If others cheat to get ahead, I need to as well. If others take drugs to succeed in sports or academically, then we have to take drugs too. If others bribe to get their kids into "a good school," then we will bribe too. If others control people by hot topic religious ideas, we need to find hot topic secular ideas to control people also. We are a world of cheats, and those falling behind are the ones who can't or wouldn't cheat. Some can't cheat because of the rigged system and others don't know how to for no one taught them. Some wouldn't cheat because their conscience prevents them.

In every transaction, there is a winner and a loser. However, even worse, the winner often asks, "what is the maximum they can get out of a transaction?" The winner does not consider how the transaction will impact the loser. We feel the need to squeeze as much as we can from the loser while telling ourselves, "don't leave money on the table." We are experts at self-justification. We believe that making just enough profit on an exchange is never good enough. As a landlord, I have raised the rent just because I could. I thought, "everyone else in the city has raised their rent, I must do likewise to keep up."

I remember an incredibly painful episode that taught me the lesson that we are all cheats vividly. This happened when I took my 75-year-old father to a cardiologist. The cardiologist after having carried out three tests and finding nothing, wanted to perform one more test. That last test was not only useless, it was harmful to my father and to his dysfunctional kidneys. The cardiologist said to me, "if I were in your shoes, I would have my father do the test." This is a line straight out of a sales "how-to" manual. Upon hearing his words, I became suspicious. After asking a few more questions, I realized that the result of that newly proposed test, whether positive or negative, would not change the cardiologist's recommendation. He recommended a particular ink test because it's what was best for him and his pocket, he was not concerned with my father's health, only his bottom line. I was thoroughly disgusted walking out of his office that day. "In 2018, the U.S. spent 16.9 percent of gross domestic product (GDP) on health care, nearly twice as much as the average OECD country. The second-highest ranking country, Switzerland, spent 12.2 percent." (Tikkanen and Abrams)

Why did the cardiologist feel these tests were needed? No other reason than Medicaid would pay (never mind the harmful effect the ink would have had on my father)? other doctors write prescriptions for brand name medications, when generic ones will do, or write a combination prescription when two separate medications will do. They are all looking out for "number one" and doing the best for themselves, which according to our society is the best for everyone. It's commonplace now to be vigilant when you visit the mechanic or the car dealership. However, what does it say about our society when now in addition to the mechanic we must be wary of the cardiologist and dentist as well?

What is left of a community when even the ones who swear to do "no harm" can be so blinded by money that doing no harm is secondary to making a profit? Was a fourth test better for my father? Was the fourth test better for Medicaid and the taxpayer? Of course not, yet we love to tell ourselves that many of our actions are the "best" for everyone not recognizing we are causing harm all around us. I am not intentionally picking on doctors. My own uncle is a great and caring doctor and there are many wonderful doctors in this world. The point is if even doctors, who are amongst the most conscientious of us all, can cheat so openly by following the philosophy "greed is good," how would that affect the rest of us, what are we capable of? Would we be able to recognize how we are harming others to get ahead? If we realize that we are causing harm, would we even care? Need I speak of lawyers and corporate executives and the biggest cheats of them all, traders and bankers on Wall Street? We can all easily recognize the harmful effect of that cardiologist's overt selfishness, but what if there is a more destructive selfishness that we don't acknowledge and what if this disguised selfishness is the cause of most of our problems in the modern world?

The result of all this overt selfishness is that we have plenty of cheats at the top who unintentionally or intentionally cheat the government (and that government is us). Governments around the world play a sick game with corporations; they compete with other governments for corporate tax dollars (a side effect of competition we conveniently ignore). Even after corporations come back to a country, governments struggle to get them to pay any taxes whatsoever. This is the case with the majority of the US's most profitable companies.

> *The 379 profitable corporations identified in this study paid an effective federal income tax rate of 11.3 percent on their 2018 income, slightly more than half the statutory 21 percent tax, 91 corporations did not pay federal income taxes on their 2018 U.S. income. These corporations include Amazon, Chevron, Halliburton, and IBM. An ITEP study released in April 2019 examined 2018 Fortune 500 filings released to date and found 60 companies paid zero in federal income taxes. Now, all companies have released their 2018 financial filings, and this report reflects that. Another 56 companies paid effective tax rates between 0 percent and 5 percent on their 2018 income. Their average effective tax rate was 2.2 percent.*
>
> Corporate Tax Avoidance in the First Year of Trump Tax Law

We again see the results of our competition if Company A uses a certain loophole to get out of paying taxes. Then Company B, to compete, has to do likewise. So, governments compete by lowering taxes and corporations compete by dodging taxes, an ever more downward race to the moral bottom of behavior. Here is what our government is teaching; a father teaches a child to be an excellent thief, and then when he is grown, that father is surprised that his student is stealing from him. So, the father asks the son, "how could you steal from me? I helped you grow and introduced you to my friends and protected you when others wanted to harm you and this is my reward?" And the son answers, "father, you reap what you sow." Wiser words have never been spoken. "We reap what we sow," in a genuine sense, is the point of this book. We reap it in advancement, in economics, in politics, and in mental health. Bad ideas have harmful consequences, and a small awful idea adopted by all has enormous consequences and socially destructive effects. What do we reap when we sow "greed is good"? We reap corruption: corruption in business, corruption in politics, corruption in education, corruption in healthcare, and finally, corruption in our courts. But worst of all, it is all legal corruption. Legal crimes are far more destructive, far more insidious than illegal crimes. When legal corruption is so rampant the cry will come, and it's here. Who are you to tell me not to steal $1,000 when you let others steal billions? Who are you to tell me not to cheat ten people when you allow others to cheat tens of millions? Who are you to demand that I follow the law when you let others break hundreds of laws and commit innumerable crimes?

TWO

Law of Gravity or Law of Morality

ACTIONS OF GREED HAVE CONSEQUENCES, similar to jumping out of a window. If we jump down from two feet, it will not cause much harm. If we jump from ten feet, we will most definitely feel it and probably break some bones, yet we will probably live. If we decide to jump from a thousand feet, we don't get the opportunity to make that mistake again. By the same token, all eight billion of us are as one, causing harm because we are greedy. Those selfish actions may not seem to matter much. Perhaps some die from a prescription drug epidemic, or we might fill our prisons with nonviolent drug offenders for the sake of cheap labor. Those actions will not end all 8 billion. Dreadful actions will matter more when many die from lack of water and wars. Yet here in America, we are happy and who cares what happens to those who are not American citizens?

Performing medium acts of greed causes a financial crisis or even a pandemic like the recent Covid-19 outbreak. Such disasters will harm far more people. Now the old insignificant "them" has become the significant "us." The root cause of most problems is either a desire to get more money or a desire to save more money. Both are the result of greed, and greed is only the outworking of pride. For example, we could have mitigated Covid-19 much better if China had been transparent regarding how bad things truly were. Why were they not transparent? because they wanted to hold onto power. Why do they want to hold onto power? Because being in control brings in lots of money. It doesn't matter whether Covid-19 started in a wet market or a virus lab; greed let it out. (C. S. Lewis, Mere *Christianity*, 1952)

As for the United states, when President Donald Trump was asked why he eliminated pandemic oversight posts. He replied: "some of the people we cut they haven't been used for many, many years... rather than spending the money, I'm a business person I don't like having thousands of people around when you don't need them." That response could be summarized as the desire to save money. It always comes down to money. There will come a much bigger problem if we continue along this path. These problems will be akin to jumping off the thousand-foot-high window. Just like the pandemic is unmanageable now, no matter the amount of money the US government throws at the crisis after the fact, we will face something we can't manage. Unfortunately, when disaster hits, we will not have enough time to create tools or acquire enough knowledge right then and there to meet the challenge. By then it will be too late to take advantage of the billions of brains and life experiences we have on this planet. Being able to rely on a small number of highly educated people is better than none, but it is insufficient in meeting the challenges of humanity. By not allowing ordinary people to have enough life experiences, we jeopardize our future with our greed. Mr Taylor put it this way in his book Weapons of Mass Instructions

> *On April 13, 2008, John Kanzius appeared on television to discuss a heretofore unknown method of killing cancer that had been invented by a patient with no background in science and no college degree. Nobel Prize-winning cancer researcher Rick Smalley said that it was the most impressive development he had ever seen in his life, that it "would change medicine forever.*
>
> *The Kanzius Method destroys tumors without chemotherapy, surgery, or familiar radiation. After 36 rounds of chemo, John Kanzius was desperate enough to wrack his brains for something which the cancer empire had missed, he found such a thing in memories of his boyhood hobby as a radio hobbyist. As a kid, Kanzius had been intrigued by a curious fact: that when harmless radio waves passed through metal, the metal heated up. Was it possible that a tumor injected with metal particles could be killed by passing radio waves through it? Ridiculous idea, isn't it? Had it merit, surely the army of trained scientists who cost the nation tens of billions every year would have found it, wouldn't they?*
>
> Weapons of Mass Instructions 2008

Our lives are a mosaic of experiences and in destroying that mosaic of experiences, we ruin American society, our country, and our world. Greed is constantly destroying that mosaic, by poverty, meaningless escapes from reality, or by a constant pursuit of pleasure. These all are self-destructive and are marketed and sold to the masses for a few to become ever more prosperous. All those factors destroy the mosaic of our existence and leave us wide open to not locating the likes of Kazius the next time he might be desperately needed.

On the other side of the planet, greed is playing the same melody, only there it has more friends. Chinese society can't withstand the assault of greed and oppression for long. The greed of the CCP (Chinese Communist Party) is evident by the fact that it pockets 50% of all government R&D (research and development) and other project expenditure. Through its American enabler, China is laying the foundation for another war. This war might be cold or otherwise, or the greed of the whole earth bringing about climate change. From the likely results of this greed, or something new, there might be no coming back. Greed is always the problem and never the solution. Never forget "we reap what we sow," every action has an equal and opposite reaction. Sometimes the opposite reaction takes a while to be fully realized, say fifty or sixty years, such as with the decline of America. The equal and opposite reaction always comes. We can see both likely realities coming our way now, and averting either reality will require monumental effort.

We all want what's best for us. That will never change. We create laws to civilize human nature, but laws can't keep up. In reality, laws are falling farther and farther behind. How long will we focus on the symptoms and not the cause? Some would say "it's not that bad, we have changed the world. We have the internet and smartphones; poverty is declining and world-peace is on the rise." Things have improved despite the system not because of it. We could have done it better all along, capitalism is no longer the main reason we have a better world. Improvements occurred because of improvements in morality and education, in its inception capitalism itself was an advancement in morality. When we decided the king does not get what others worked hard for that was a great leap in moral improvement, yet the larger a system gets the more moral it must become. As capitalism is now a global system it needs another moral revolution. As the world becomes more stratified the same old model reveals its shortcomings more and more, the developing world advances, to the detriment of the lower and middle class of the developed one until now we started a race between countries on which society can handle more oppression the longest as Branko Milanovic put it in *Global Inequality*:

> *In short: the great winners have been the Asian poor and middle classes; the great losers, the lower middle classes of the rich world. Such a bold statement may not surprise many people today, but it would certainly have been surprising to many if it had been made in the late 1980s. Politicians in the west who pushed for greater reliance on markets in their own economies and the world after the Regan-Thatcher revolution could hardly have expected that the much vaunted-globalization would fail to deliver*

palpable benefits to the majority of their citizens – that is, precisely to those whom they were trying to convince of the advantages of neoliberal policies compared with more protections welfare regimes.

Branko Milanovic, *Global Inequality*, 2016

They bore the brunt of the losses while the top 1% raked in the gains, till we reached obscene levels of inequality. If the wealthy's desire to help is genuine, we would have seen the wealthy become less wealthy, and the lower and middle class take a more significant portion of the economic pie.

THREE

Right or Left

My point is not that America is a lousy country. On the contrary, I think America is one of the best countries to ever exist. Yet the fact is we can no longer control the cheating, corruption, and, more importantly, our abusive economic system that supports, cements and even encourages legal theft and oppression.

Every generation should endeavor to be better than the one before. We will only become better when we examine where we went wrong and find our way out of the echo chamber of corruption and self-delusion. No country can survive long with this level of legal corruption and indifference.

The consensus among scholars and historians seems to be that most of the American decline began in the 1970s. There is no agreement on what happened in the 1970s that started America on this slippery slope. However, it is well documented that the average American's life has been deteriorating on almost every metric since the 1970s. Society has reached such new depths, now we are looking at the next generation, which according to the Research Center will make less money than their parents (accounting for inflation), work harder than their parents (working two or three jobs), have a less satisfying family life than their parents (a direct result of working too much), and experience more social and mental illness than their parents. Deterioration at every level: family life, hours of work, number of people who work per household, cost of education, pay after graduation, prospects for retirement, health-care affordability, and upward mobility all have consistently declined for 50 years. We refuse to see the situation, or perhaps we are too busy to notice. A tapestry of decisions began eroding society in the 1970s, chief among these phenomena was the explosion of computerized trading, and then later, the internet. Such perfected systems of greed and convenience cost us dearly. They force businesses and society to make ever greater sacrifices to mechanized greed, offering up more and more to appease its new god. Only, it will not be enough for our new god wants it all.

What happened in the 1970s that started us on this road? Some think it's globalization, poorer quality education, or drugs. Others say that we simply stopped going to church and became "bad" people. In reality, it's likely this is the result of hundreds of decisions and small steps made by previous generations, which lead us to our current predicament. Ideas and actions have consequences, no matter how much we attempt to mitigate or ignore those consequences, the harmful results of bad ideas are unavoidable. Real improvement comes from changing our ideals, not mitigating the consequences of flawed thinking.

FOUR

Keep or Exchange

We all dream of the day when 90% of Americans own their own homes. A day when families are healthier, and children are loved and valued. We dream of a country where people work 20 hours a week instead of 60 hours a week to make a living. It would be an America where we feel fulfilled at our jobs. We dream of an America where we have time for each other and for relationships. We would hope it to be a time when the family is strong once more.

The sad reality is that we are headed in the opposite direction. We are headed into a "nightmare America" where 10% of people own all the homes, an America where children get fewer and fewer opportunities. We are headed into an America where work is ever more meaningless, and to make a living you must work 80 or 100 hours a week. A new America where friendships and healthy families are as rare as payphones and the mystical eight-track tape.

How long will it take for us to recognize the failures of our economic system? If you buy a new car, and at first sight it looks great and runs well, but after a week of use it's completely useless and dead, you might naturally take it to the dealership to be told: "don't worry, it needed a minor new part, now it will work great." Then the car works great for another week yet soon dies again, at which time you once more take it to the dealership. You are then told "don't worry now we got it. We will give you a new battery, this time it will work great." Only the car breaks faster than ever.

Four days later and the car is back to not working. How many times should you accept a new part as the solution? At what point should you think to yourself, "I want a new car, forget about fixing this one, it's a lemon."

We have had three major financial crises in the last 20 years, how blind we must be to continue this way. By the same token, at what point do we recognize that it's not the people who are the only problem, but the system is irrevocably broken? The idea that "greed is good" can only take us so far, and it's continually warning of its inability to get the most out of "the battery" we call humans. Capitalism is trading in our humanity for goods, and that's the dearest trade we have ever made. Yet, we continue to exchange our lives, not for each other but for a better car or a bigger house. Republicans and Democrats, rich and poor, Christian and atheist decry "the battery" and still love "the car" They rail against each other and love capitalism.

Can we stop blaming people for the faults of capitalism? Can we realize that Republicans are not the problem, that the poor are not the problem, that the atheist or Christians are not the problems? We have good and bad people in every group. More importantly, we ourselves are capable of great extremes. So that the same person who harms sometimes heals and the best healers can cause great harm. It all depends on our choices, our environment, and the lessons we decided to live by. After rising to the top of capitalism, some individuals saw the mess we were in and tried to fix it. Chuck Feeney comes to mind. But even Feeney's giving away all of his vast fortune will not be enough to change the world. Also, Feeney and people like him are the exceptions not the rule. For every Chuck Feeney, there are 50 or 100 other billionaires on the other extreme who are happy causing havoc in order to become ever richer. The rule is "the rich will get richer." This is simply the only truth about capitalism. The truth about capitalism is not only that "greed is good" which most of the world believes. Even worse, we believe it now more than ever before since we have been repeating it to ourselves and to each new generation. We mindlessly repeat this same mantra as if it's the truth when in fact it's just a warped distortion of reality.

> *A reliable way to make people believe in falsehoods is frequent repetition because familiarity is not easily distinguished from truth. Authoritarian institutions and marketers have always known this fact.*
>
> Daniel Kahneman, *Thinking, Fast and Slow* (2012)

What if we decide to stop believing in this falsehood? What if we stop believing the "Gospel of Greed"? What will happen if we choose not to attempt yet another fix to this lemon of a system and we decide we need a new monetary system instead? We could decide that we need a "car" that does not require a new "fix" every few years. Things will be different with a new working "vehicle"; maybe then we can change the world, perhaps then more of our potential can be reached.

Some great inventors who wished to change the world never got the chance, for those in power preferred the status quo. Such inventors could not or would not cheat to compete. For example, in the 1900s, Nikola Tesla imagined wireless communication and wireless charging, more than 100 years before we had this technology. Our best sciences have yet to make all his dreams come true. Mainly because of the "Gospel of Greed," he could not compete with Thomas Edison. By all accounts, Edison humiliated Tesla in numerous ways. Tesla was a great inventor and we enjoy his inventions to this day." A dozen reliable sources had told Brisbane that 'there was not the slightest doubt about his being a very great man.' 'Our foremost electrician,' people said 'Greater than Edison' " (Tesla Barnard Carlson 21). All that and yet Tesla died destitute. He would not cheat to such an extent that "Westinghouse went to Tesla and asked him to give up the contract and help him retain control of the company. According to O'Neill, Tesla then tore up the contract in a grand flourish, demonstrating his loyalty to Westinghouse" (Tesla Barnard Carlson 207).

What kind of world would we have had if Tesla had been helped more and marginalized less? Between Tesla and Edison, who do most people admire? Who do most people quote and know? Of course, the answer is Edison. But who would you teach your children to be more like? Whom would we say was "the better man"? The answer is clear: Tesla. I acknowledge that we have to cheat, that is what we call profit margin. How good of a cheater a company is usually determines their profit margin. In a real sense profit is the way we reward creativity and effort, it's what makes our world better. However, without profound changes, Netscape could never compete with Explorer just as Tesla could never compete with Edison. That lack of true competition is a major hindrance to progress.

Here is where the government steps in to even out the odds. The government intervenes when there is a significant imbalance of power between the players. This makes sense, for without this assistance, Netscape had no chance against Microsoft. A referee is needed to make the game fairer. Judges are hard to find for the average person. Good lawyers are even harder to afford. My intention with this book is to be the average man's lawyer. I'm no doubt a poor substitute, but any defence is better than none. You may ask: Why do we need a lawyer for the average person? Doesn't the government look out for their rights? The government has a hard enough time looking out for its own rights. They seem to need more help than they can give. Governments around the world are losing to corporations. Some might see the current world stage and conclude, if corporations are so bad, maybe the way China is doing it is the best way.

China's tight control over the sharing of information and their oppressive system will never work, nor should it. It's setting a terrible precedence; it is taking a massive step in the wrong direction. The Chinese system of controls and their attempts at hindering the flow of information and free expression are devastating to the human psyche and costly to the world, as we are learning from the Covid-19 crisis.

Furthermore, China cannot improve their system, it can only degenerate from here. When the foundation is wrong and self-examination is disallowed, the building will fall no matter how intense the internal support is. Their system is irredeemable. Furthermore, those who supported China externally in terms of offering education or investment are culpable in all their actions. Fortunately, I moved to America and not China when I was 13 years old. Mercifully, I'm in a country where saying "you are all wrong" will not land me in jail, or worse. It's mind-boggling to me that many of my friends see no difference between the United States and China. They defend their moral equivalence in order to support the equality of the two sides' worldviews. The only conceivable reason for that kind of behavior is a misunderstanding of Christianity and of our history. This misunderstanding has created a profound rejection of Christianity and a desire to attribute the west's rise and freedom to anything but Jesus and the New testament. In a desire to equate people we make the profound mistake of equating ideas when in truth the best way to help people is distinguishing between ideas.

No one yet knows the best way forward. However, we know what does not work. Censoring people and ideas do not work. Having absolute monarchs does not work. Having pure capitalism or pure communism does not work. All our current "vehicles," do not work because they are all lemons that continually need fixing. They need fixing with wars, with laws, with uprisings, with great depressions and great recessions, with central banks, by printing more money, and other equally harmful monetary policies. These fixes are harming 95% of Americans to help 5%. The more we "fix," the worse capitalism gets. Take for example the last stimulus, out of $3 trillion, only $1 trillion is going to the people (which is better than none). However, those people will turn around and hand most of it directly to the wealthiest 1% of the population. This will only exasperate and widen the wealth inequality. There is a bug in the car and adding parts or changing batteries will not remove the bug.

The bug starts with us, not with capitalism or communism. The bug is the fact that we all want to be first (pride is in all our hearts). We want it so bad we will do anything to get ahead. As John Kenneth Galbraith said: "Under capitalism man exploits man. Under communism it's just the opposite."

In this book I aim to find a new way, and admittedly, even with a new system there is no doubt man will find ways to exploit others, but it will be much harder. Yet just as capitalism is regarded as better than communism, this new way will be better than capitalism. In communism, the power of government is extreme and in capitalism the power of corporations is extreme. Even worse in capitalism the government has been gaining strength in order to match the growing power of corporations. Such undertaking is a recipe for disaster.

The new way will cut both institutions, government and corporations, down to a manageable size. Even though we know man always exploits man, many reading this will not see themselves in such light. We only see others as immoral. By the end of this book you will realize we are all selfish. Some of us are overly selfish like that cardiologist. At least we can all agree his actions were "harmful." We all practice and let others practice a different form of disguised selfishness that no one mentions. We all do it and so we think it's ok. Since it's performed by all it must be good. This is a little like a gang of pirates, none of whom will tell the others they are immoral since they are all pirates. Or imagine a group of slave owners, none of whom will point out the ugliness of slavery since they are all slave owners. Even to the point when one slave owner says to the others "slavery is immoral" the answer was always "judge not lest you be judged." It's often the guilty who tells others not to judge, using pseudo-logic to justify their own awful behavior.

I expect that many people reading this have the sense that our lives should be better. In 2020 we should not be making the same arguments we made in 1950. If anything, we seem to be going in the opposite direction. We are constantly getting farther and farther from each other. With all this technology and computing power, why have we not been able to do better? One hundred years ago, Republicans and Democrats agreed on laws and passed bills together, but now it's surprising if one Republican or one Democrat agrees with the other on any law. Are we that different now to how we were then? How does a morally rational person look at the world and not agree with another moral and rational person on a way to fix anything? Is America so perfect that there is no need for new laws to improve our country? Or is the list of problems so long that we can't even agree on where to start? I believe the answer is self-evident.

Some decry our lost morality, and others rail against our lost potential, and yet others focus on our lost connections. Why are we coming apart at the seams? Both Charles Murray and Robert Riech have laid out a grim future for America, and that grim future is looming over the entire world. It's not that Americans are worse than the rest of the world and because of that things are so bad. Rather it's because we have had our "car" the longest and it's only now starting to show some severe signs of wear and tear. We have been a capitalist country for many generations and during that time we have frequently needed to fix this system to keep it going. In short, we were here before. In the 1920s we had the same extreme inequality (which was also preceded by a flu pandemic) and we had no solution then either. The only catalyst that pulled us out of that era's extreme inequality was a world war and a massive increase in taxation, as solutions now one is undesirable and the other is unimaginable. We had a choice 100 years ago (and we failed miserably to make the right choice), and we find ourselves in the same situation again. Can we get it right this time? Many saw these problems and predicted our current location. However, we have failed to avert this runaway inequality from once again becoming our reality. It is now here and more of its consequences will follow if we fail yet again. To understand how the 1920s got to be so bad, we must look back even further, back to Charles Darwin and the Theory of Evolution from the year 1859.

With Darwin's rise, our overt and disguised selfishness has been emboldened, reaching a crescendo in the 1970s with Richard Dawkins' "the selfish gene." This Idea has been with us since ancient times, from the first writing of man. However, recently our selfishness and its consequences have been given new life thanks to Darwinism and later Richard Dawkins. We are now free of all moral restraints. Selfishness is now the highest good along with greed, pride, and whatever else any shrewd biologist, psychologist or economist can convince us to believe is part of human nature for there is on more good or evil. After all, it's because of our greed we have gotten to this point in our human development. If using greed got us this far, it must be good and we must continue on the same path. Here again I must use the slavery example, for the West advanced in significant ways precisely because of slavery. However, that in no way made slavery good, moral, or right. Instead, slavery forever tarnished the advancements of the West. By the same token, greed forever spoiled the recent progress of our society. The ends don't justify the means, yet we humans let it do so all the time. That disguised selfishness coupled with our economic system will doom us all. Private inherited wealth is the disguised selfishness. Just as those slave owners of old never wanted to let their slaves go, we don't want to let our modern "slaves" go. Rather, we have gone the other way; many then gave themselves permission proclaiming that it's their right and good to own more slaves, now we echo their sentiment and say it's our right, and even beneficial, to be ever more selfish.

As a consequence of the "death of God," many now see the world differently from what was the norm 150 years ago and this evolution is not for the better. We now have "a dog eat dog world." Remember, "A reliable way to make people believe in falsehoods is frequent repetition. This is because familiarity is not easily distinguished from truth. Authoritarian institutions and marketers have always known this fact" (Daniel Kahneman, *Thinking, Fast and Slow*, 2012). That belief is turning our world from a jungle into this nightmare place we call a "dog eat dog world." When all we see around us are cannibalistic dogs, and only they alone are "fed and full," we will conclude that in order to be fed and full we also must become monsters. The more monstrous, the better you become at competing for the ever-dwindling prey (some call them customers).

When others rebuke the cannibals saying "you should not be a monster," the answer will simply be "if others turn into cannibals to compete I must as well to keep up and compete at their level." The cycle will never end.

Now we come to a place where we exalt in our vileness, some call them profit margins. Factually, dogs do not eat dogs, instead dogs care for one another better than many humans. Even wolves work together knowing that they must cooperate if they hope to succeed in catching the prey. We have twisted the narrative of the jungle to justify our ill-logic and immorality. Most leaders only see a dog eat dog world, and it will doom us into becoming just like that. Just as in *Oedipus Rex* the king ensured his own death at his son's hands by believing the prophecy that his son would kill him, our belief that our world is "a dog eat dog world" will ensure it becomes that eventually.

In America, we have witnessed years of preying on the weak. Now we have become divided, angry, resentful, and, worst of all, we don't know why we feel this way. The rest of the world is quickly following in America's footsteps. The world is following without the constraints of morality that the American elites used to have. Without a standard we are all just the blind following the blind and we know where they will both end up. This is what has caused a man called Tarek el-Tayeb Mohamed in Tunisia to set himself on fire as an act of protest. That man sparked the flames of discontent across the Arab world and those flames burn hot to this day. Only instead of an easing of the load, nations have been burdened more than ever before.

What has taken Americans 100 years to get to, the Arab world and most other countries have achieved in half the time. What will wake us up? What are we waiting for? Are we waiting until some poor soul set themselves on fire in our own neighborhood? Aren't many following that path here already? It took many years for the elites of America to break free from the yoke of religious constraints. The rest of the world's elite are achieving this in a much faster and crueler manner. Now, nations are coming to the boiling point quicker than ever before, all as a result of the "Gospel of Greed" and its marriage with moral relativism. The moral relativism of the rich and academia coupled with the philosophy that "greed is good" is the ultimate self-destructive force, and that combination will soon deal our society a mortal blow.

I see it every day. I see it when people don't have the funds to get medications, or cannot put their kids in good schools, or even find enough food to eat. I hear it from Egyptian engineers and accountants working 12 hours a day, six days a week just to keep up with basic expenses. I hear it from Mexicans when I visit their country. I see it playing out in our lives here in America every day. I hear the struggle in the voices of my fellow Americans when I endeavor to help them with health-care insurance. If they can afford the insurance plan, they can't afford the deductible, if they pay the deductible, they can't afford the monthly bill. I read and hear many intellectuals who are experts at diagnosing the symptoms of our current crises, but when it comes to the cure they are tongue-tied. Economists and politicians have a long list of symptoms but they can hardly write a few words about the treatment.

Would it be too bold to state there is hardly any area of US society that we can point to and say that it has improved in 50 years? Rather, almost without exception, our society has deteriorated. Crime is the only area of exception, but only because we have filled our prisons to the brim, to the point that we have become the world's number one in numbers of incarcerated citizens. And now Americans turn the guns on themselves instead of each other creating the highest suicide rate in American history. What does that say about the American political and economic elites and where they are leading us? What grade should they get for this leadership? Is a higher GDP all that is important to the American elites? Are we in a factory of 350 million employees? In this factory the more we squeeze out of every worker, the happier the boss gets. If America is not exactly this way yet, then we are definitely headed in that direction. Republican and Democrat writers see the myriad of problems, but when the author comes to their cure, I find myself deeply dissatisfied. For the past 50 years, or even 150 years, the two sides have always made the same arguments. If doing the same thing for 150 years and expecting different results is not the definition of insanity, then I don't know what is. Since I no longer consider myself on either side of the political coin, I feel it only right to state my side.

How many times have we raised the minimum wage in the United States? How many times have we changed and created labor laws? How many times have we lowered taxes? How many times have we relaxed regulations? How many times did we expect the "new solution" to change things and it has not worked? All our problems from the little cheating in "mom and pop" stores to the monumental cheating that goes on in corporations, banks, and Wall Street are because of greed. Our laws can't keep up and will never be enough. Neither will watchdog groups effect enough change. A fundamental change is needed or we will keep finding ourselves in this situation again and again until we learn or until we put an end to learning all together.

Another way to look at it is to imagine we were required to solve for X in an equation and for a century we have yet to succeed. If the equation is nonsense, it does not matter if a quantum computer worked on it for another century, it will remain unsolved and unsolvable. This "Gospel of Greed" is that equation, and for 300 years we have been trying to "fix" it only for it to get worse after each "fix." We have written book after book hoping to solve for "X," but it hasn't yet been solved. Each side is confident that their value for "X" must be the correct answer. It's time we stop solving for "X." The equation is unsolvable. After 300 years it's glaringly apparent that something is missing in this equation and there is not enough information to solve for "X." The right-leaning answer for "X" says we have to lower taxes and make the poor better people, and the left-leaning answer for "X" says we have to raise taxes and make the rich better people. Neither the rich nor the poor can improve for both are living with the philosophy "greed is good."

We feel we have no choice, if we want to survive in this jungle, we must become even more greedy. Let's open our eyes and find a new way to get ourselves out of the fix our awful ideas have put us in. However, in this book I will not talk about taxing income more or less.

Once I stopped using pseudo-logic and I decided to look honestly in a mirror at myself and not at others, then I began to see myself for who I really am. And with a clearer view of myself I saw us all.

As a salesman I used to close many sales by the words "that's only fair, right?" As humans we understand fair, we like fair. Being fair and being logical are two sides of the same coin for the human mind. We all understand we should be fair. However, for generations we have been blind to true fairness. We are bombarded by a cruel world yet do little to nothing to fix it. In America we have been allowing the world to get ever crueler, once more we need to learn what it means to be fair.

For centuries, some have enslaved others, for decades men have refused to let women learn and grow, now we look back and ask ourselves: "Did they not know that was unfair?" Could they not see how awful they were being, and how come the slaves did not rise up against that system? Did they not know that they were depriving their own countries of the much-needed contributions of blacks and women? However, we were slowly able to come to the realization that fairer is better. We constantly need to learn what fair really means. It is such a simple idea yet we have trained ourselves not to recognize it. We consistently need to remember that fairer is better, for we love our pride. We come into this world and are immediately indoctrinated. We are instantly blinded to the consequences of our actions. It is not until we have people who rebuke us for our immorality, that we manage to wake up from our self-delusion. I sincerely hope that waking up this time will not require another conflict.

The most advanced society is the fairer society; they are one and the same. We can never have equality of outcome, but we must have equality of opportunity. For a century, many saw the slow, and inevitable return to the current inequality we see. For a century, economists could see where the trend was headed in the US and around the world and they did nothing. If anything, they helped the inequality along by reducing taxes on the rich, and on capital gains, and giving corporation tax loopholes and allowing corporations to have stock buybacks. The excuse always being that we need to compete with other nations and we can't let others overtake us. Even after all the sacrifices we made, we are still being overtaken while some bask in utter comfort. In reality, these austerities cause the American decline: greed added to indifference will never lead to a better country. Slowly it gets worse for its citizens and worse for its standing in the world.

What will our country look like in a century from now if things stay the same? This question assumes we will survive another century which is actually a monumental assumption. What kind of financial gulf will exist between the rich and the poor in that timeframe? Will our grandchildren talk about the top 0.00001% instead of the 0.1% we currently discuss?

Will America be a better country after we stop counting our billionaires and start counting our trillionaires? Some might think so, but the truth is I would rather go back to the days of monarchs than forward to a day where trillionaires exist. For at least a ruler felt they had more responsibility to the average person for they were a political leader. But now economic leaders, thanks to Milton Friedman, have a duty only to their shareholders, and everyone else be damned. However, it will not just be everyone else who is damned but those very same leaders who think themselves insulated from harm.

We all know that economic elites cannot change since they have to continue to compete. Many people believe that we must tax the rich more, but that will not change the outcome, it will just delay the inevitable, and may also make America less competitive, leaving the likes of China to expand its influence. This is a prospect that many proponents of democracy don't cherish, given China's history and recent actions. We are in a fix and it will be extremely challenging to move in either direction. The reason we are in this position is not because Americans are bad, but because capitalism is slowly changing us, forcing us to turn more hideous and we hardly notice. Communism became progressively worse until its people despised it and fought against it, capitalism has turned progressively worse until its people despise it and fight against it.

To compete with others, we must become more vicious. Ultimately, whilst competing with an authoritarian regime, America will become an authoritarian regime. Life in the seventeenth century when Adam Smith wrote *The Wealth of Nations* is nothing like life today. What people did for jobs and education is nothing like what we are living and studying now. How they lived has no resemblance to our lives now, and yet the way we order our societies has been the same, with little change over 300 years. Since Milton Friedman's theories influenced the West's economic policies over 50 years ago, instead of dialing down the pressure, we have turned up the heat. As if greed were not bad enough, we decided to add indifference, proclaiming two wrongs will make a right. Can we cease from repeating the mistakes of the past 50 years or will we continue while expecting new results? Is it time to say we can't solve for "X" because the "equation" is missing crucial information? Will we recognize that both sides are right and wrong about "X"? Is it time yet or is another 50 years of misery necessary to acknowledge our failure? Is our society dysfunctional enough for us to decide we need a significant change? For some inexplicable reason, we believe we are improving as a country. However, if we examine any metric, we are digressing. Just because our technology is improving does not mean our society is improving also. What is the point of technological improvement if it's destroying our happiness and society?

Some imagine that in the near future we will magically create something better with artificial intelligence (AI). However, looking at all indicators, we will likely degenerate into something which is decidedly worse for the overwhelming majority of humanity. Technology is not the problem; it's our human heart we must fear. What did humans do with some of the earliest computer programs? They traded on Wall Street, even now the most essential cornerstone of computer advancement is concerned with how to use algorithms to make money from money. In other words, take money from others, and what is taking money from others called? The answer is stealing. Don't think I'm upset that I lost $300,000 on the stock market and because of it I'm against trading (I'm no longer upset and just like golf or chess, the only person I can be upset with is myself and I have decided to forgive myself and move on). It's just that I realized taking money from others creates nothing, adds nothing, improves nothing. Much in the same way that the first act of a computer program was professional theft, so will the first act of general AI be professional theft. Just as computer programming was first used to take from others on the stock market, GAI will be used to find ever more sophisticated ways to do the same thing.

Once any of us has an advantage, we always use it to lord over others, from the creation of bronze weapons to cyber warfare. After we perfected the automobile, we had World War I. After we perfected the airplane, we had World War II. Now as we perfect technology we are headed into a new nightmarish world. People are suffering a tremendous amount of pain in America and around the world and the cannibals are oblivious.

I suspect that computerized trading more than anything else is the reason that, from the 1970s onwards, America had started to fail. America is now so dysfunctional that we have a system where creating is not rewarded. A person might be better off becoming a sophisticated thief on Wall Street than anything else.

Taking such actions may transform that person's life for the better, yet it will make America worse. Americans need traders as much as a human needs a tapeworm. After 50 years of having a tapeworm, we now wonder "Why is the patient so anemic?"

We have become so anemic that it's now impossible to ignore the problem. What about modern society has gotten better? Has mental health improved? No, it is much worse. Has marriage improved? No, as an institution it is almost completely destroyed. Our children's lives have become increasingly more miserable, they are constantly needing more drugs to cope with modern life. Our communities are crumbling. Americans feel lonelier than ever before, even prior to Covid-19 hitting. The idea of having a healthy work–life balance is the inside joke of most job interviews. We are systematically destroying everything that a good society means and the sick joke is we are laughing and smiling through it all. Do you think eight people owning as much as the bottom 50% of the world's wealth is a sustainable system? And our outrageous answer is a universal basic income, most of which will go straight to the landlords and the top one 1% cementing the inequality even more. How blind must we be if we think this gross inequality is tolerable let alone beneficial?

Can we decide to cease from repeating the same actions over and over while expecting new results? Is it time to say we can't solve for "X" since the "equation" is essentially incomplete? Can we recognize that both sides are right and wrong about "X"? Is it time yet or is another 50 years of misery required to acknowledge our failure to solve this problem? Is our society dysfunctional enough for us to decide we need a major change? For some inexplicable reason, we continue to believe we are improving as a country, but by every metric, we are digressing. Just because our technology is improving, it does not mean our society is simultaneously advancing. Society has done nothing, but become worse for the last 50 years. As a matter of fact, rather than becoming better because of technology, our technology is a major part of the reason why our society is crumbling. Those at the top will still look at themselves as the liberators of humanity when in reality they are humanity's jailers.

We have mental suffering, familial suffering, societal destruction, and financial exhaustion. The saddest fact of all is that we brought all of this upon ourselves. I hope we are ready to take the next step, it will not be easy: improvement always demands a deer cost. But stagnation will cost much more.

FIVE

Jungle or Garden

MORALITY IS where this book actually began. It's where I struggled with myself in the search for truth. At this point, I must mention my parents, who each in their way showed me reality. My father pursued truth and justice even if declaring it harmed him. My mother demonstrated mercy and compassion even when doing so harmed her. Through their examples and my searching, I have stumbled upon the dual nature of morality. This truly was the most incredible discovery I could have dreamed of. It does explain most of what we do and why we do it. This concept of the dual nature of morality is not new, nor is it mine. However, I have tweaked it in a way that allows me to see myself and the world differently. I was not looking for a new way to run the world but a new way to run my life. After all, capitalism has been good to me, so I had no desire to change it or look for something new.

Have you ever wondered why we have this duality

everywhere? We have a mother and a father, a left and a right side of the brain, capitalism, and communism, Republicans and Democrats. Why are there always two sides? Why not three or five? The most we ever do is fuse capitalism with communism to create the monetary system we all use now; namely socialism. Every country uses socialism to a different degree. Some are capitalist-socialist, such as the United States, others are communist-socialist, such as the old USSR. Yet still, there are just two directions: either the capitalist avenue or the communist way. Because we only have two ways of thinking, we either think help "us" or help "them" one may seem more moral than the other, but it's not. This, however, did not start with politics; for me, it began with Jesus.

The Christian argument

Morality for me started as it does with any pastor's kid growing up in a Christian home back in Egypt. It began with Jesus's words in the sermon on the mount and with its more condensed version of the good Samaritan.

> *And he answering said, Thou shalt love the Lord thy God with all thy heart, and with all thy soul, and with all thy strength, and with all thy mind; and thy neighbour as thyself. And he said unto him, Thou hast answered right: this do, and thou shalt live. But he, willing to justify himself, said unto Jesus, and who is my neighbour? And Jesus answering said, A certain man went down from Jerusalem to Jericho, and fell among thieves, which stripped*

him of his raiment, and wounded him, and departed, leaving him half dead.

Luke 10:27-30 (KJV)

When we hear these words, many of us automatically imagine their impossibility. Not only that, we balk in suspicion at any who try to live in such a manner as if they are incredibly dense not to live for themselves and themselves alone as our society teaches. Furthermore, when Jesus was asked, who is my neighbor? Jesus answered with the eternal example of "the good Samaritan" – a man who saw his enemy on the street and decided that he would not treat him as an enemy but as a neighbor. However, that story is not an example of what we should do to our neighbors; rather it was an answer to "who" are our neighbors.

What some of us do is act like the good Samaritans and think to ourselves: "Since I acted as the good Samaritan a few times. I did what Jesus said; I loved my neighbor as myself." However, that again is pseudo-logic.

Jesus was not asked: "How do I love my neighbor as myself?" if the question was "how" acting like a good Samaritan would be sufficient, but the question Jesus was asked is: "Who is my neighbor?" to that question, which Jesus simply answered, "everyone is your neighbor." Let's not deceive ourselves just because we do what the good Samaritan did a few times, does not mean we are following Jesus' commandment to "Love our neighbors as ourselves." "Who" is a question of persons, "how" is a question of action.

We are not following the commandment, not even close. Furthermore, we can never live up to it in a capitalist system. Capitalism can never coexist with the ideal "love thy neighbor as thyself," just like the "Gospel of Greed" can never coexist with the Gospel of Jesus. One must destroy the other.

To follow Jesus' words, we need to both love ourselves and love our neighbors equally. What does Jesus mean by this? How can we do both equally? The least Jesus meant by love, is to help, so we can say, help my neighbor as I help myself. Can we do that in capitalism? Is there any chance that I can help others as much as I helped myself? Again, in capitalism, it's impossible. But with one change, we can help all Americans as we have helped ourselves. In that way, we can inch closer to the goal of following the greatest teacher who ever lived, and in that way, we can transform our world.

As our country has left the teaching of the Bible behind, we have slowly drifted into this inaccurate view of the jungle, a view that goes something like "it's a dog eat dog world" or "might make right." This belief has harmed us all. We all have held onto this disguised selfishness for such a long time and it's time to let it go, for that disguised selfishness is destroying our world.

For 4,000 years, the Bible has warned against the rich, their actions, and against greed. Jesus did not have one positive word to say about the rich, and yet in some churches, we love the rich and want to be them. How can we have anything else but crumbling society as a consequence of such hypocrisy? It is self-destructive. It's what we deserve for calling evil good, and good evil. Ask yourself why Jesus said:

> *No man can serve two masters: for either he will hate the one, and love the other; or else he will hold to the one, and despise the other. Ye cannot serve God and mammon.*
>
> Matt 5:24 (KJV)

Daniel Bell in *Cultural Contradictions of Capitalism* echoes Jesus' words in saying "the unbounded drive of modern capitalism undermines the moral foundations of the original protestant foundation." Where Bell uses the word "undermine" I would use "obliterate."

It's either the "Gospel of Greed" or the Gospel of Jesus. If you love one, you hate the other. If you hate one, you love the other. For when the bible says:

> *the Love of money is the cause of all evil*
>
> 1 Timothy 6:10 (KJV)

We might ask, but what about homosexuality, and abortion, God? What about "all" do we not understand? Is it time to listen to the Bible? Other evils will be solved if we solve the love of money problem first. The majority of self-destructive behavior that people do in society is a direct or indirect result of capitalism. The order of steps one takes to solve a difficult problem is crucial. Trying to solve abortion by legislation will always be met with failure if we continue to ignore the most prominent cause of abortion: lack of money. The slow drift in society is a direct result of a lack of community which in turn is a direct result of a lack of finance. Some might think economics and community have nothing to do with each other. In truth, they are inseparable, as an individual lives to work all other considerations slowly fall away. There is no community between impoverished or overworked individuals. The moderately rich still has communities, however the poor get to suffer more and do their suffering in isolation. (Alienated America)

Jesus did not talk about homosexuality or abortion. However, he had the harshest words for the rich and the lover of money. He said that the rich will hardly enter the kingdom of heaven (Matt 19:23 Matt 10:23). If a person thinks that they can be a Christian capitalist, they either don't know what Jesus said or don't know what capitalism is, or worst of all, they know and don't care as long as they are benefiting from the inequity. We must rotate our perspective of the self and unto the neighbors, we must teach "do the best for others and it will be the best for the self."

Some in the American Church do the exact opposite of what Jesus did: forgive and love the rich and scorn and condemn the harlot. In short, those who live and teach that way are the Pharisees of our time. Worse yet, we have found the person who loves money the most and we have appointed him as our leader. Every time we elect a Republican in America, disaster follows. Shortly after George H. W. Bush was elected, we found ourselves at war in the Gulf. Later George W. Bush came to lead and during his time in office we saw 9/11, two wars, Hurricane Katrina, financial crisis, and skyrocketing debt. Now, we have Donald Trump and the result is the Covid-19 pandemic, soaring unemployment, and unmatched national debt coupled with government chaos and incompetence Now we are on the brink of a race war. We seem to be incapable of realizing that abortion is not as harmful as the love of money, just like the Pharisees refused to acknowledge that obeying the Sabbath and not healing was worse than breaking the Sabbath in order to heal. We too need to learn that God desires mercy not sacrifice.

If you think Republicans are the lesser of two evils, it seems God does not agree. God says the love of money is the cause of all evil and the new American church replies: "No God! You're wrong! The love of money is the cause of all good." We go on spreading the "Gospel of Greed" to the whole world and expect no consequences. Others have called evil good before us and God already responded to them:

> *Woe unto them that call evil good, and good evil; that put darkness for light, and light for darkness; that put bitter for sweet, and sweet for bitter! Woe unto them that are wise in their own eyes, and prudent in their own sight! Woe unto them that are mighty to drink wine, and men of strength to mingle strong drink: Which justify the wicked for reward, and take away the righteousness of the righteous from him! Therefore as the fire devoureth the stubble, and the flame consumeth the chaff, so their*

root shall be as rottenness, and their blossom shall go up as dust: because they have cast away the law of the LORD of hosts And despised the word of the Holy One of Israel.

Isa 5:20:25 (KJV)

God has given us free will and with our free will we can choose our destiny. Individuals, countries, or the whole planet can even choose to take their lives but we can't blame anyone but ourselves, for the law of cause and effect can't be broken. It's not clear when Christians lost sight of "the problem of the love of money, but it's about time we see it again. There is only one example for the Christian to follow.

Look not every man on his own things, but every man also on the things of others. Let this mind be in you, which was also in Christ Jesus: Who, being in the form of God, thought it not robbery to be equal with God: But made himself of no reputation, and took upon him the form of a servant, and was made in the likeness of men: And being found in fashion as a man, he humbled himself, and became obedient unto death, even the death of the cross. Wherefore God also hath highly exalted him, and given him a name which is above every name.

Phil 2:4-9 (KJV)

Do we want to be like Jesus or would we rather take the Pharisees as our role model?

The evolutionary argument

Some might say, "I accept that Jesus said to love your neighbor as yourself, but I don't believe in Jesus, or in religion at all so why should I bother with that?" We should bother because there is no other way to live, or survive. We all want to advance, just as we want to help others succeed. The apes do not survive alone. Apes don't have useless leaders who sit idly and expect to be served. The ape who leads, is also the most useful. Often, the one protecting the group the most, or the one hunting the best, becomes the leader. No leader in the jungle is a useless or abusive leader. Yet, we have many such abusive leaders in our modern jungle. Dare I say as a result of competition, no one has risen without some kind of abuse of others. Ours is a system that would never have been tolerated in the real jungle. We are so accustomed to harming others of our kind in our modern jungle.

Other than during times when their survival depends on it the question to ask is, do animals eat their own? Rarely do apes act in such a manner. Apes and wolves are examples of social animals who care for their kind deeply "...to the point that an ape lost his life trying to save a baby ape whose mother was especially careless" (Frans de Waal, *Primates and Philosophers: How Morality Evolved*, 2016). To my astonishment, Frans De Waal has done much research that directly supports this book's conclusions. De Waal starts his book *The Age of Empathy* (2019) by stating, "greed is out, empathy is in." It's encouraging to finally see evolutionary psychology catching up to the most basic of Christian ideals. However, it is ironic that the same ideology that gave birth to the "dog eat dog world" way of living is now trying to right the ship. No doubt, it's because some recognized the direction such ideas are taking us. Nevertheless, better late than never.

Regardless, the evidence points to morality as the basis of why we do what we do. Morality and motivation are forever intertwined; this book asserts that our monetary system and the way we have structured it are the cause of our increasingly crumbling society. It asserts that capitalism supercharged with moral relativism is forcing us through the mechanism of markets to override our inherent moral behavior and act more savagely towards one another. Again, to compete I must use whatever advantage I can find even if it harms others. When it comes to my advancement or the advancement of others, I will most often choose to favor myself rather than others if my society makes it an either-or choice. My goal in writing is not to condemn Darwinism or Christianity or any other philosophy. The fact is that ideas have consequences and whether we are Christians, Muslims, Hindus, Buddhists, or Atheists or anything else, we all grew up adhering to a harmful idea that needs to change. Capitalism has been making humans behave worse for 250 years and the deterioration accelerated in the last 50 years.

Elon Musk and the Wachowski sisters (creators of the matrix) posit that we are in a simulation. I agree wholeheartedly, the simulation is our reality. We choose in the simulation: take the blue pill or the red pill. That is the choice we make over and over in our lives, to harm (ourselves or others) or to help (ourselves or others). One way will lead us to an ideal existence. The other may end all life. In this simulation, there are only three truths:

- There is an ideal state.
- We consciously want to reach the ideal state.
- We subconsciously want to reach the ideal state.

Those are the only facts about our reality. Right now, we are far from the ideal state, which is nothing new. The real concern is in the last 50 years we have been rapidly moving farther from the ideal state. We are masters of self-illusion; we see degradation at most sides and call it progress.

The overlap

The question of morality has haunted me for years. Why is one thing better than another? I framed it to myself this way: why are the Nazis so bad? (A question Mr. Ravi Zachariah asks often.) Most would agree that Nazis are evil, and we should never have a Nazi society, but why? The Nazi party wanted to advance and bring forth "the super-man" that Nietzsche claimed we desperately needed. They wanted to help humanity on its evolutionary path to greatness, bringing along a world full of superhumans, smart, and tall, all-around better than the rest. On the surface, inspiring ideals (if they were not, millions of the most educated and rational people on the planet would not have followed it). The question we need to ask is: at what cost? Not dissimilar is the future Yuval Harari envisions for humanity in "homo deus", only where Nietzsche saw an over-man Harari sees a god-man. One must ask before it's too late: at what cost will this god-man appear?

Becoming better is all well and good but who will we harm on our journey to perfection? Many of us have a goal, and we are taught to say to ourselves, "I will reach my goal no matter what." I was repeatedly taught this lesson in sales. Nazi Germany also had a goal, which was "a better world." The most educated people in Europe at the time were going to "help the world" become over-men if they wanted it or not. The Nazis were going to civilize the savages and make humanity reach its goal, and why not? "The ends don't justify the means." Just because their goal was good – namely an over-man – it doesn't mean the method was right. Having a noble purpose is not a license to do whatever suited them to get to that world. The Nazis wanted to acquire their version of a better world by killing millions. Out of harming others, we will never create a better world. No matter the intention, out of harm will always come war.

How is our greed any different from the Nazis' harm of others? It's only different in degree but not in kind. The Nazis severely harmed others to advance by use of murder, medical experiments, and other human atrocities. Capitalism harms others to advance as well. The harm capitalism causes is not as gruesome as slavery or the Nazis but there is no doubt 200 years from now (if we should last that long) our descendants will look at us with the same pity and moral outrage we currently have for the defenders and perpetrators of slavery or the Nazis. We justify the harm we do in capitalism similarly to how Americans justified slavery 200 years ago. Whether it's through evolution or Christianity, man always finds a way to justify his most outrageous action: collective willful blindness that we tend to fall into no matter the level of education or perceived societal advancement. We say, "we are only harming others a little in order to advance." After all the Nazis killed to advance, all capitalism does is raise the rent without needing to. Raising the rent without needing to is less wrong than murder. But it is not less immoral if the goal is not to harm and capitalism also has a cumulative negative effect. Remember, the end does not justify the means. Capitalism may not harm Americans much at the moment but it has destroyed many other countries and an incalculable number of lives.

Every transaction harms someone, either the seller or the buyer, the benefits are never equally divided. We justify ourselves by saying, "I'm not killing them," but even then, we are wrong, for we are slowly killing someone's dreams and hopes, and the poorer a person is, the shorter their life expectancy is. It's impossible not to transact, but again we must be honest with ourselves if we have any hope of advancement. Sometimes the winner is the buyer of a product. For example, if a person buys a book or a smartphone for the first time, they get access to new information that can't possibly be equal to the price of the product.

We like a "win–win" situation, since it's the most

moral concept we have. "Not only do I advance, but you will advance also." In essence, we tell each other that there is no one being harmed in the transaction. Working in sales I know the term "win–win" is often used and never true.

As a race, we know that being fairer has always worked to our benefit, it was not fair for the monarch to own all the land and use 85% of people as their slaves, also known as "peasants." It was not fair that black people were enslaved to whites. It was not fair that women didn't get equal rights and opportunities to men.

Even monkeys understand the concept of fairness, "they reject unequal pay for the same work 50% of the time and unequal pay where one monkey does not work at all yet gets a reward 80% of the time" (Sarah F. Brosnan & Frans de Waal). A great sense of fairness made us gather together and share our food instead of killing each other as hunter-gatherers. Apes look for fairness in their leaders. For if the alpha ape is abusive, he will not be alpha or around for long (Frans de Waal).

We are continually re-discovering that the most moral behavior and most useful behaviors are the same. Jesus said, "It is more blessed to give than to receive." Acts 20:35. And the latest happiness science states, "if you want to be happy, it is better to give than to receive" (Elizabeth Dunn). Even in sales it's proven that asking someone to do you "a favor" makes them like you more, for it causes them to like themselves more. We are happier with ourselves when we see ourselves as helpful toward others. We all revolve around those twin desires. The twin ideals of helping myself and helping others, improving myself and improving others, loving myself, and loving others. The idea of giving is demonstrated in the elderly's increased desire to help others since the end of life is a hard mirror to avoid. We decide, "I helped myself enough; it's time now to help others" (yet some are trying hard to avoid even death, and with it the mirror that death represents).

This book will be the mirror for those who refuse to see themselves, for we all must examine the depth of our depravity. There are many good moral teachers, but as you can tell, Jesus is all I need. He is the greatest psychologist, economist, and philosopher there is. Once again, I will repeat what he said: "love thy neighbor as yourself." That is the only Truth we have in this world. Do we need to wait till psychologists and economists agree that the way of love is better, or should we wait until they tell us that it's the only way forward? Just like happiness has to do with giving rather than receiving, an idea that's been in the Bible for 2,000 years, can we afford to wait another 1,000 or 2,000 years before we realize that the only way forward is not a "dog eat dog world?" Can we even last another millennium with such an abhorrent philosophy?

Love is the only way forward. If love is the highest ideal, why do we continue to believe we will create a better world without it? Worse still, we believe glorifying the antithesis of love will help bring us together. Some ignore morality because they feel science is more useful. Science is incapable of rescuing us from ourselves. Science is a double-edged sword, with it we grow food to feed the hungry, but also by it we bomb those whom we just fed. Everything we humans come up with is that way since that's how we are. We can either help or cause harm either way, we are becoming better at both. Science is remarkable only when scientists are helpful, but science could quickly become terrifying, as it did with nuclear weapons in World War II or now as it builds the surveillance state of China.

The way of greed turns us into cannibals, tormented, angry, and full of regret. We may be useful to ourselves and society, but often after a person becomes "rich" they turn. If cannibals have friends, they are usually other cannibals: who can abide by their presence or who can stomach their behaviors, who can risk trusting a cannibal. If they are not physically alone, they are most definitely mentally alone and that's when it's necessary to pay others to keep themselves from feeling loneliness. We are turning into a world of smiling, laughing cannibals exalting in what we should be disgusted by.

Do you think monsters see themselves as such? Of course not. I will tell you how I know. When I was a "little monster," I never saw myself as such. I never even bothered looking at a mirror. Furthermore, if you are not well off now and think to yourself, "I will not be a monster once I'm rich," the chances are you will be the same or worse than the rest. Seeing our flaws is near impossible. Remember how we treated African Americans for hundreds of years. Also consider what we are still doing to black people. Remember how we treated women for decades. We are always the hero of our story and never the villain. Only a tiny minority can see their monstrosity. Fewer still see the effects of their actions and admit to themselves the harm they are causing. We are experts at excusing the harm we cause to others. For example, I used to justify my cruelty by saying if I don't cause harm, someone else will cause it. If I don't buy a house and evict the current occupants, others will buy the house and evict them regardless. But do such arguments work in reality? All such ideas are nothing more than self-justification. If we were in a jury of a rape case and the argument of the defense was "I raped her because if I did not the next guy would have done it and I was the gentlest rapist," what verdict would the jury pass down? Guilty of course. Rape is rape; it's the action that is wrong, not just the intention. Do we want to live in a world where what others might do justifies us, causing harm? Unfortunately, it's already too late; that's our world, and only when we have an overwhelming number of acquittals for rape will enough people wake up to the modern rape culture we live in. Actions are right or wrong because of the harm they cause not the perceived intention of other parties.

Religion used to be our mirror. However, most in power have refused religion. Most have tossed it aside consciously or subconsciously, for better or worse. It is not something the elite have time for anymore. Nor do they use it to look at their behavior. Most of the world's elite prefer science to religion and I tend to agree, it's better in the case of the material world. However, when it comes to the immaterial world, such as human interaction, science is useless. It has been utterly harmful. It's used only to excuse our worse actions, always in the name of advancement. When it comes down to how we should treat each other. We are only now catching up to the most elementary Christian ideas.

Now, research scientists are telling us, just seeing the money from the game Monopoly has adverse effects on how we treat each other. Monopoly money turns us from normal kind humans into self-absorbed, inconsiderate people. So much so, we can measure its impact on our behavior (Vohs, 2015). What do you think "real" money does to us? If Monopoly money is so powerful, then real money must be more powerful. If seeing it affects us so, then holding money will necessarily affect us more. I shudder to imagine the effect money has had on the human psyche. Generation after generation, these monetary systems of dog eating dog are stripping us of our humanity. It's been happening for 50 years. It is slowly changing us in order to avoid a revolt, but our change will come at a much higher cost than merely a revolution.

Is money bad? Money is a tool we use, since we can't do without it. Like any tool, its usefulness depends on what purpose we give it. We can decide to build with a hammer, but others might see a hammer only as a weapon. For thousands of years, money has been seen as a weapon. The usefulness of money is hardly considered. All we do in this neoliberal cannibalistic system is make money from money in which nothing new is created. There is little to no thought of relieving the oppressed, quite the opposite. All they do is press the olives more to make their oil. This system is continuously looking for more olives to press domestically or abroad. Just as we use nuclear power to either help or destroy ourselves, we have been using money in its most destructive form for generations. We have gravitated towards using money to harm as quickly as we drink water, especially in the last 50 years. Money should be a tool by which we encourage the most useful among us. But as "dog eat dog" capitalism took over the world, money became less and less a tool and ever more a weapon. Now, it's more than a weapon; it's our overlord. Our new task-master, driving us to greater and greater levels of cruelty (some call it income inequality), for we hate looking in the mirror. The more we sacrifice to money, the more sacrifices it will demand. This will happen until we have people starving in the wealthiest country on earth and in response, we are shrugging our shoulders in indifference. We just don't see it as all that bad just as our ancestors did not see that monarchy or slavery was terrible. It's how the world is after all and who do you think you are for changing the world anyway?

The way to fix capitalism is to follow exactly what Jesus said 2,000 years ago. We all have two guiding stars in our lives. Recognizing the two stars helped me navigate through life much like our ancestors did thousands of years ago. Working out those two moral ideas are where all our conflict comes from. After a lifetime of searching, I found that those two moral ideas govern all my behavior.

Before stating the two principles. I'm warning you not to fool yourself. Here they are.

Do the best for me without harming anyone.

Do the best for others without harming anyone.

As I have switched allegiances between being a Christian or not, between being a Republican or not, between being well off or not, those two ideals have always been there. Now, did you fool yourself after reading this? After reading the two ideals did you think to yourself "I should do the best for the largest number of people?" If so, congratulations, you have deceived yourself in the same way that most of us do. "This is the essence of intuitive heuristics: when faced with a difficult question, we often answer an easier one instead, usually without noticing the substitution" (Daniel Kahneman, *Thinking, Fast and Slow*, 2012).

We all quickly want to substitute the challenging two ideals into a comfortable one ideal way of thinking which we can follow. We fight among ourselves because of the simple trick that our minds have played on us for generations. Those two sentences can never be combined. Those two sentences will only ever get farther and farther from each other (see Figure 1 below). Helping myself will always lead to harming someone and helping others will always lead to harming myself. Now, even though the harm can be slight enough as not to matter. There is still someone being harmed.

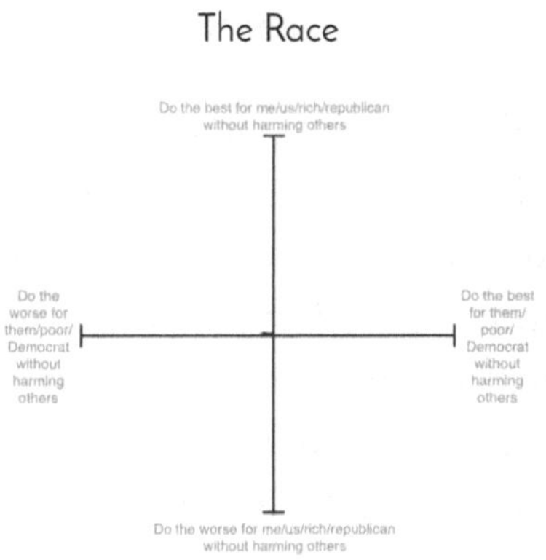

Figure 1

LET's think back to old cartoons where you had a devil and an angel on each shoulder. What does the devil always say? He says "do what's best for you!" What does the Angel always say? "Do what's best for others!" Except for a few, no one wishes to harm. What we desire is the best for ourselves, and if it causes harm. Then we retort, "oh well, shit happens." After all, we cause harm every day to many people, and we can't eliminate all the harm we cause so we blind ourselves to it instead. We will come back to those two principles many times in this book. These two principles have revolutionized my life and transformed my view of the world and I hope that they do the same for you.

This is how immoral capitalism truly is. Imagine you're in a race, everyone is lined up and ready to run the race. Hard work and IQ represent our two legs. Some start the race a little ahead of the others; some start the race a little behind. You are happy you get to start closer to the front. You notice a few ahead, but not many. Suddenly, you look at the giant screen showing the finish line, and what do you see? The giant screen shows millions of winners partying at the finish line. You think to yourself, "that's odd we haven't even started the race and they already won? How did they start at the finish line? I did not get a chance to run yet!"

Naturally, you ask the referee, "excuse me, but what are all those people doing at the finish line? That's not fair!" The referee replies with, "well, they have a different race they need to run that does not involve you. Just mind your own business. You thank the referee and think, "well life is not fair, but I will do my best." as Dr Kahneman puts it in *Thinking Fast and Slow*.

A reliable way to make people believe in falsehoods is frequent repetition because familiarity is not easily distinguished from truth. Authoritarian institutions and marketers have always known this fact.

The referee starts announcing the rules of the race. You are ecstatic. You figure he would say "let's have a clean race, no shoving, no tripping." However, He instructs "shoving is encouraged, tripping is allowed. The runners who pass the finish line are going to make it their mission to hinder all the rest from getting past the finish line." As if that's not bad enough, he next states "everyone that crosses the finish line will cause the line to move farther away. So, the first hundred runners who pass the finish line will have run a 100-meter race but after the

1 billionth runner crosses the finish line, the race has turned from a 100-meter dash to a 100-mile marathon (100 years ago passing the fifth grade guaranteed a good life now getting a master's degree is often not sufficient.)

Once people hear the rules, they get discouraged. Some get discouraged and decide, "forget it, I am not even running." Others think, "man, I'm going to go get a bicycle and ride my way past these rule-following idiots." But they are usually caught and disqualified from the race. Nobody ran a race before, and all figure that this is how races are run. Some are at the finish line encouraging us by saying: "you can do it." They motivate others saying, "look I started at the very end and now I'm here." They fail to tell you that they would not let their children start the race from the very back again, let them encourage their own off-spring with such proclamations. They also know the rules and understand that the finish line is ever moving farther away thus. This makes it harder for anyone to cross. Everyone that crosses the finish line gets to help make it harder for others to cross. How do you like this race? I bet it would be fun to watch. It would be exhilarating to see all the tripping and shoving, as I am sure you can imagine. But watching is one thing, and participating is another. Some are upset with the ones that will not run. Others are upset with the ones getting a bicycle. And yet others are upset with the ones born at the finish line. Some are extremely angry with the referees, but even the referees do not know any better. They have always had the same rules. I'm most frustrated with the rules rather than the runners or referees. No one is happy in this race. I know most of us believe that the people partying past the finish line are happy. If anyone has a choice, of course, that is where we want to start. Regardless, we are moral creatures and knowing consciously or subconsciously that we cheated to get where we are has consequences. Knowing we are doing nothing except hindering others in order to live even better lives has its effects. But that effect is nowhere near the impact that is had on those who have been getting obstructed all their lives.

We all know that such a race is repugnant, we all know starting at the same line is the only way to race, and yet we let the most important race of all, the race of life, become more and more unfair every day, usually because the winners make the rules. Consciously or subconsciously, they will never make it fair for they are firm believers in the "Gospel of Greed."

It's the hard runners the rest of us who must stand up to this insanity. We must rewrite the rules of this miserable game for most are "blind to the obvious, and we are also blind to our blindness" (Kahneman). Jesus put it long ago this way.

> *Therefore speak I to them in parables: because they seeing see not; and hearing they hear not, neither do they understand. And in them is fulfilled the prophecy of Esaias, which saith, by hearing ye shall hear, and shall not understand; and seeing ye shall see, and shall not perceive: For this people's heart is waxed gross, and their ear are dull of hearing, and their eyes they have closed; lest at any time they should see with their eyes, and hear with their*

ears, and should understand with their heart, and should be converted, and I should heal them

Matt 13:13-15 (KJV)

Fairness is at the heart of what we do and who we are. Some would say it's a jungle: the strong win and the weak die. What's new about that? I would respond that the jungle is much fairer than modern society. For the jungle is inherently fair. The race in the jungle is much more just. We can only dream of an opportunity to turn our society into a place that equals the fairness of the jungle. What should we compare our society to? The communities of monkeys or lions, or some might prefer wolves. Feel free to use whatever mammal you wish; their morality has surpassed ours by miles, for in all those kingdoms two facts are always present. Every animal starts at the same level, for they can't construct all the shared narratives that we do: my electronic money, my corporation, my copyright etc. Also, if our society was like their society, then a person only advances by helping others advance and by showing their strengths and abilities. Many train to instruct the poor. If a person wants to be rich, they would have to work hard for it, pull themselves by their own boot straps and become rich. That's where the original American dream came from. The idea is to come from nothing and become a self-made millionaire. That may sound fair but it's only fair if and when everyone gets to start from the same line. Why don't we tell those born as billionaires to pull themselves up by their own bootstraps? Why is pulling yourself up only demanded of the born poor or middle class, yet not required of the born wealthy?

You become the pack leader because you're the best and strongest hunter. Being the strongest, you help the most in bringing down prey, and in defending against attacks (Jordan Peterson). We violate both rules and fool ourselves in thinking we are acting in a just manner. The kingdom of man is full of undeserving kings, kings who install their children as our princes, and we have allowed such abuse for generations. Just as peasants of old who adored their kings, we in this modern world adore the abusive rich as if they are our model, when the only rich we should cherish are the useful rich. Most of our current elite are the abusively rich and they have no business being wealthy, for they are harming far more people than they are helping.

The result is instead of coming closer to the rules of the jungle, we are continually going farther and farther away from it. Instead of becoming egalitarian, we turn back the arc of progress and return to the days of a monarchy. Instead of rewarding only the producers who help the majority, we reward both the individuals who benefit and harm the majority and then we wonder why so many are harmed. We see no distinction between the useful rich, and the abusive rich. As a society we must create a way to distinguish between the Steve Jobs of this world and the far more common Jeffrey Epsteins of our country. They were both billionaires, yet each has the opposite effects on our society. It's necessary to encourage those who do the best and dissuade those who do the most harm. The harsh truth is often the same person who did the best starts to cause a good deal of damage. How do we stop them from getting too corrupted? It's not that they are especially bad, we would often act similarly in their shoes, it's just the ugly side of human nature magnified under the telescope of capitalism.

Let's take another example, one that's near and dear to my heart. Chess is one of the oldest games ever played. If a game can be said to be fair, then for sure chess is. Yet, white always goes first. go figure! However, despite this, chess is a great game to use as a blueprint for life. Everyone starts with the same number of pieces and gets an almost equal chance at winning.

Are our lives like chess matches? Does the loser of a chess match get angry with the winner? Does he refuse to play him again? Just the opposite, as the loser of many chess games, I can tell you I love playing more capable players. Stronger players make me better at the game. If I get mad, I usually get frustrated with myself for playing dumb. A dear chess opponent of mine always says, "there are no stupid moves, just stupid people." I might still lose the chess match, but I will have learned something from my loss, and the one thing that I can never say is "that game was unfair." It could be called challenging, it could even be described as impossible for me to win, but it could never be an unfair game. Are our lives like chess? Far from it. If our lives are like chess, then I start with a king and three pawns, and others begin with a king and 15 queens.

We have many players who think themselves chess

grand-masters when in reality, all they have done is win an impossible-to-lose game. Let's take the best chess player of all time, no longer a human, but a Google AI called DeepMind; let's not give it three pawns but eight pawns. Will the best chess player ever be able to beat a child who has 15 queens? Of course not! In this lopsided chess match, we find the same kinds of people.

Winning in this lopsided chess match, is no different from winning in the lopsided race, the winners think themselves "great runners" when all they did was be born at the finish line. Some see this and don't even bother playing; others decide to break the rules while others give it their all (even though they are hopelessly outmatched) they still try to win. The hard workers say to themselves, "if I work harder, my son will have three pawns and two bishops and certainly that's better than what I started with." For the other side, it does not matter; they will now add two more bishops, for they always make more of an employee than they pay them.

History is written by the victor. In capitalism, the rich are the victors, and they have written the rules. The "rules" have increasingly favored the wealthy, and now we are at the stage where most people no longer want to play their sick game. It's not that others are lazy or dumb or inconsiderate. It's that the game is so repugnantly fixed, and the losers are now smart enough to notice how monstrously the cheating has truly become. The tricks will no longer work. The rich can only cheat as long as the poor are oblivious to their antics. Thus, the purpose of proper education is reserved for the few to allow the few to "manage" the many.

The system only works in one way, which brings us to how I harmed to get where I am. How an immigrant who started with nothing, barely even speaking English got to live a relatively good life. So much so that I could make/borrow $300,000 to lose in the stock market and still live comfortably. The answer to how anyone rises is they must perform harm against others. I'm one of the best "three pawns" chess players; others taught me how to play. I got a college degree, which helped add a few pieces on my board, not as many as you would think. What helped put a few pieces on my board was being a good salesman. Also, when I got to play other "three pawn players," I would get a few pawns from others like me. Most of these people were bad players and I could beat them. Did I think about the people I took chess pieces from? Sometimes I did, but the justification was always "if I don't take these pieces, others will."

I bought all my houses from "bad players," those in bankruptcy or those who lacked the means or time to fix up their home, and sell them well. Did me buying a house, fixing it up, and selling it mean I'm a bad person? Of course not, yet I can't ignore the fact that for me to rise, others must fall. If anyone feels tempted to state "it's not a zero-sum game," I would like to take this chance to assure you it most definitely is, it just takes decades or centuries to balance the equation. I fixed the houses and I spent time and effort and money turning them around, yet none of that changes the fact that for me to rise, others must fall. Capitalism has gotten people so accustomed to harming others; most are oblivious to the consequences of their actions. It's time we admit it; someone is always being harmed either internationally or domestically, regardless where in the world the losers are, the fact will never change, if there are winners, then there must be losers. Crushing the weak players even more until they have nothing might seem common, but it's not right, and once you create a majority who start with just a pawn and a king soon after you will have a war or a revolution. People are happiest in countries that have the least wealth inequality. It's not the wealth gap itself that makes them unhappy (Richard Wilkinson, *Spirit Level*). The game's unfairness makes them despondent, even if some don't know how to articulate the problem. Nonetheless, they know something is wrong and their subconscious is aware of the reality even if their conscious mind can't verbalize who is cheating them. That's a significant reason why a con man became president. Most cons convince you that others are after you and only the con man is the safe harbor. Since the American elite are in-fact stealing and manipulating the poor and middle classes, it was not hard for Donald Trump to convince enough of the population that they were being cheated. For in the assertion that someone was a thief, Trump did not lie, only the cheaters are not the Mexicans as he claimed.

How many people would refuse to play a rigged game? Would you play an opponent a game of Monopoly when they start with double what you have? How about 100 times what you have? How about 100,000,000 more than what you have? Would you still feel like playing? if you must play, will you take it seriously? Of course not. What's the point? Fairness is at the heart of all we do. Aren't all personal arguments just dialogue of fairness? When two parties argue, they always disagree on what's fair. That is why we observe the two sides going farther and farther back in time in their disagreements; it's a practice of self-justification. Let's use a metaphor of two chess players to illustrate this: we end our matches 2–1, my opponent might say "two days ago I won 3-–0, so for today you won but for the week I'm ahead." To that I respond with "a week ago I won 3–0 so for the week you are ahead but for this month I'm the winner." This goes on and on, until we are discussing the matches we played five years ago. We do the same in marriage going farther and farther back to prove we are the true victim.

Each side getting what is fair is how we run the world. From lawyers to salespeople, between parents and kids, from national trade talks to national wars, it's about what each party thinks is fair. What has everyone who ever cried unfair in history received for a reply? "Get used to it, life is unfair." But life is not inherently unfair; it's just that we have convinced ourselves that it is and we have allowed an ever-increasing number of people to play billions of others for fools.

A reliable way to make people believe in falsehoods is frequent repetition because familiarity is not easily distinguished from truth. Authoritarian institutions and marketers have always known this fact.

Daniel Kahneman, *Thinking, Fast and Slow, 2012*

We then ponder the source of anger and resentfulness. What is resentment but thousands of little perceived or real acts of unfairness that build a wall of hate and anger around one's heart?

I hope by now, you agree the most moral way is to start at the same starting line. I hope you realized that playing chess and winning because one party is starting with 15 queens is no great feat. Instead, succeeding in that manner is a hollow victory. By now, I hope the questions you are asking are: How do we do it better? How can we all start at the same place? How is it even possible that we all start a chess game with the same kind and number of pieces? I will answer those questions in later chapters. What's important at the moment is not the how, but the why. The why is far more critical for we all know "where there is a will, there's a way." Only victory against an equal opponent counts as a real victory, and other kinds of "victories" are hollow. They are at best, useless and, at worst, destructive. The truth is that most of the victories in America now are just that, hollow victories of 15 queen players against three pawn players.

The more we advance, the farther Republicans and Democrats will end up from each other, until they are so far apart that we will split this great country over it (we almost did this once before).

The North wanted to free the slaves, embedded in that desire is the ideal "help others without harming anyone." Of course, it was going to harm the South and the South wanted to help itself. Included in that want is the ideal "help myself without harming anyone." Of course, they were harming the slaves, so the South held on to the pseudo-logic that black people somehow did not count under the "don't harm anyone rule." That they were not the same as Browns, reds, whites or yellow, the consequences of that idea are still haunting us today. In all of human history, our conflict has revolved around those two ideals. To my knowledge it had never been put in those terms before, Regardless, that is what we did. When the first tribes of humans attacked their neighbors, they did not do it out of hate but out of necessity or envy. They did it out of the need to improve their situation and they of course ignored the harm. Now we attack ourselves and are headed rapidly toward self-annihilation of all for the pleasure of pride. The "helping myself without harming anyone" slowly evolved into "helping us without hurting anyone." Then the futility of not harming anyone became obvious to all, and it too was abandoned. Thus "we versus them" evolved from the "I versus everyone" philosophy. That is why we came up with two styles of human organization. Both fight and argue over and over again, for each feels justified in their respective ideals, always following their north star till they can't do anything but fight. If we continue along this way, the Right will fight the Left. If we continue this way the East will fight the West. If we continue this way instead of advancing, we might put an end to advancement all together.

We are trying to combine the two ideals that are

found in every human heart. We will always come up against that distinction. Wanting the best for myself financially will never magically turn into the best for others financially.

Capitalism seemed as true to Adam Smith in the 1700s as a flat earth seemed true to people in the 1500s. He thought his system worked, but now it does not. We continuously try to live up to the ideal, but now generation after generation, we are drifting further and further away from our ideals and causing havoc. The day has come to toss this kind of capitalism on the dung heap of history where it belongs. For just as it's now unbelievable that once people thought the earth is flat or that having an absolute monarch is right, it will soon be unbelievable that we thought this "dog eat dog" capitalism was ever a sound system.

We can condense Milton Friedman's philosophy into the phrase "greed is the best." He not only advocated greed; he made sure we added indifference to our way of thinking. In what now seems like a cruel joke Friedman in his book *Free to Choos*e states "Free trade would not only promote our material welfare, it would also foster peace and harmony among nations and spur domestic competition." in the face of plummeting material welfare, and rising tension with China, not to mention corporately controlled government in which both government and corporation are tone def to the needs of Americans. I can't help but recall Friedman's words, "One of the great mistakes is to judge policies and programs by their intentions rather than their results." As well as blaming the politicians, and their hollow promises we must respond with "one of the great mistakes is to judge economists and politicians by their intentions rather than their results." With a divided country, crumbling families and communities, a warming planet, and $25 trillion in debt, neoliberal capitalism true results speak for themselves. The utopia of neoliberal capitalism has become a nightmare, not too dissimilar to earlier utopia. If allowed to continue, it will end up in a more destructive manner than any seen under Stalin or Mao, only instead of millions now it's ruling over billions of newly inducted wage slaves.

During the last century, while America was going to evolve into a utopia through greed, Russia planned to achieve its utopia through sacrifice. Neither is a good standard, for both descriptions ignore the goal of "do no harm." We find that the two systems like to use those two words, for America champions greed and the USSR championed sacrifice. I will not use greed or sacrifice for they both carry an undesirable negative connotation; ingrained in both is the concept of harm. As I said, causing harm is so ingrained in us that we are blind to it. We always blind ourselves to the damage we cause. Not until the destruction caused by society's elite is so massive and intolerable will some wake up, not until a country's citizens are ready to overthrow their government, will those in power think there is anything wrong. The truth is often the more intelligent a person is, the better they are at lying to themselves and others. Few indeed who can be so self-deluded that even in the face of protests in the street, they will continue to think to themselves they are "good people."

If we want genuine improvement without harm, we should start by using better terms. Let's call the first ideal self-improvement and the second ideal neighbor improvement. Or, of course, we can decide not to reinvent the wheel and call the ideals neighborly love and self-love. The new way must be egalitarian and competitive. In *The Wealth of Nations*, the competitive models shone forth brightly, but there was little mention of egalitarianism, for Christianity was the inherited counterweight to people's greed. Doesn't America give to the poor and help people who need it? Isn't that egalitarianism? It's the worst form of it, the one form we don't want and don't need. That is not egalitarianism. An equal starting line is the only way to be fair. It's again pseudo-logic to say any other way is egalitarian all other ways are disguised selfishness.

We exalt greed and forget that what we teach the individual, we teach society. If a characteristic is not suitable for one, it's not good for all. If it's not positive for all, it should not be tolerated for any. If inheritance is not acceptable for one, namely the monarch, it's not acceptable for any. Yet, we turn around and say what is not good for a person is somehow good for all countries and for the whole world. What reprehensible logic this is. Now, everyone gets to live and bask in a world where greed is a virtue, and once greed is a virtue, societal collapse will soon follow. All this self-delusion should not be laid at the feet of Adam Smith, for it's been with us from the beginning. It's time to recognize that inherited wealth is the cause of all our problems. The apes never inherit their father's position. Only if they are useful do they get to live in comfort. Only if they can protect better than all others do they get to ascend the hierarchy. No wolf is born to the head of the pack; likewise, no human should be born rich. Inherited money is the cause of all our destruction, and yet we love that disguised selfishness so much that we again exalt in it. We hold tightly onto our greed, even as destruction looms, much like the monkey who will not let go of the nuts in the tree even as the hunter comes to take them away. We give children 15 queens and we think we are helping them, but not only are we harming them, we are hurting everyone.

SIX

Conscious or Subconscious

Life's most persistent and urgent question is what are you doing for others?

Rev. Martin Luther King

WHY DO we have a mental health crisis in one of the wealthiest countries on earth? Why are we medicating more people than ever before? Why are American jails fuller than ever? Worse still, why does America, "the land of the free," have more people in prison than any other country on earth? Why have we reached 132 suicides a day? Why do we have the highest levels of abuse of alcohol and drugs? Why is the number of single-parent households at an all-time high? At 23% it is the highest in the developed world.

What psychological problems will all that neglect leave for the next generation, and the one after that? On the whole, our society is the worst it's been in 50 years (read in: coming apart). We lead the developed world when it comes to who has the worst society (read in: Spirit Level). In fact, we could not be any worse in light of our wealth. America has gradually become an example to the world of what not to do, an example of what not to become. See Figure 2.

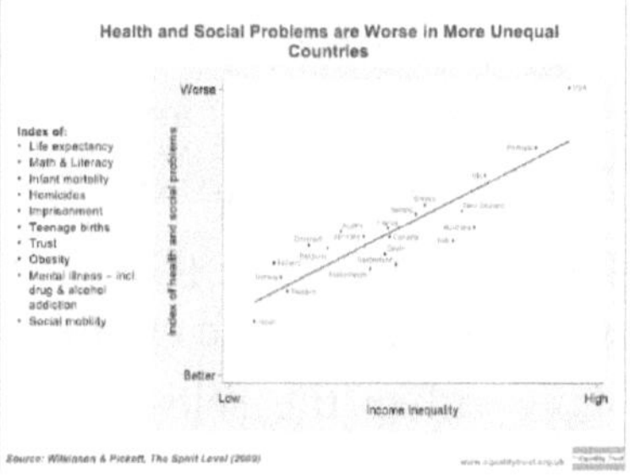

Figure 2

As this book shows societies with higher levels of income inequality have higher levels of mistrust, illness, status insecurities, violence and other stresses.

Richard Wilkinson, *The Spirit Level*, 2009

If we use an analogy of children in a school, America would be the one child whom all the other parents tell their kids not to imitate. Nevertheless, the world must imitate us since we have forced a global free market and they are obligated to keep up. We always wish to take comfort in the fact that advancements in technology and consequently GDP in America is growing, these are the highest they have been in 50 years, all at the cost of our societal cohesion, mental and familial life. GDP growth and social flourishing are in conflict, not agreement. As the wealth gap increases, our society is crumbling. As our technology increases, our loneliness skyrockets, and all we can do is blame each other.

We have always lived in a "dog-eat-dog" society. Still, before evolutionary psychology, that viciousness was held back by Christian morals (for I can't exploit my brother too harshly if I'm commanded to love him as myself). As Darwinistic capitalism began to spread worldwide, it has gradually released in us the innate cannibalistic potentials. We have to follow either the selfish gene that Richard Dawkins praises or shun the pride that the Bible condemns. As a result of this negation, we have begun to reward nearly all forms of competition with a "winner takes all" mentality in an increasingly pity-less society that turns every standard that we had for thousands of years into old antiquated ideas. What we knew to be right and good for thousands of years is now wrong and even moronic. What we knew to be harmful is now celebrated. Nick Hanauer states, "the fundamental assumptions that undergird neoliberal economics theory are objectively false. Not only are they false, but they are, in fact, in opposition to reality. It's cooperation, not selfishness, that is the cause of our prosperity."

Morality for most people has never been a set of profound personal ideals that they chose to follow closely, but rather it has simply been what has been generally accepted by society. An example of this was during slavery, whereby people "owned" their fellow human beings and kept them as slaves. The majority of that time's elites did not see anything wrong with such an enterprise. This book aims not to give the reader the complete picture of an economy after inheritance; rather, it's first aims to prove inheritance is immoral. It was impossible in one book to plot out the future off humanity after the end of slavery. First, we had to agree that slavery was morally wrong, and slowly, the world after the end of slavey began to reveal itself.

In this same manner, people see a grossly unfair system and just choose to believe that is how the world works. That worldview is the poisonous root that we have built our pharisaic and sanctimonious society upon. This moral relativity has time and again proven to be a toxic and destructive endeavor.

The root cause of many mental and behavioral illnesses can be traced to the first six to eight years of life. While some prefer to attribute behavior to genetics, it's becoming clearer that it's society and not genetics which plays a major role in shaping our personality and behavior. We quickly decided to attribute most of our actions to genes in our desire to shirk off personal responsibility. If a person is a criminal, "it's because they have the criminal gene." If a person is a cheater, "it's because they have the cheating gene." If a person is an alcoholic, "it's because they have the alcoholic gene." All this to exonerate society and the individual of all responsibility. In truth, it's mostly individuals and society that are to blame, and not genes. For generation after generation our genes adapt to our environment and our parents behavior. The first alcoholic may or may not have "the alcoholic gene." However, after many generations of alcoholics, the descendants will adapt to have the alcoholic gene. As society presses individuals into certain molds, we find an ever-increasing number of alcoholics, drug addicts, pornography addicts, and victims of divorce. An irresponsible society creating an avalanche of degradation that will be unstoppable soon if we are not careful.

A society which desires to bear no responsibility for its choices, tells an individual to do likewise. The obvious new justification now is "they were born this way. (For a good book on the subject see Steven Heine's *DNA is Not Destiny*.) We imagine we are creating a more wholesome new generation, a generation that we feel is better than all that came before. However, the statistical reality is the exact opposite. We are becoming more broken. For 50 years, this has been happening, and the trend of degradation is increasing. We are all a product of our childhoods, it takes tremendous work to identify and unlearn the wrong lessons taught to us as children.

I'm sure we all still keep the many harmful lessons we were taught as children in our heads and they are dragging us down, even now. Our task is not to celebrate our unprecedented wealth and technology, but to mourn our society and its demise. All these problems and more can be laid at the feet of the "Gospel of Greed": lack of food and basic amenities for the common man, lack of personal growth, lack of time to build quality relationships with each other, lack of time with our children, lack of connections, increased anxiety. There would even be fewer extramarital affairs if all the other areas were corrected.

Sadly, we can't deal with any of those areas; we don't have time. We have to keep running on the hamster wheel otherwise it all comes crashing down. Fewer and fewer people get to climb Abraham Maslow's "hierarchy of needs." Rather, we force more and more people to stop climbing the pyramid, stopping at "safety." And again, we wonder why our societies are crumbling. Those born into wealth have a problem with Maslow's "hierarchy of needs" as well, only in reverse. The born wealthy get to jump over the first milestones of "physiological" and "safety" needs and start right at the "love/belonging," which has its own adverse effects. When we give a child what they want without working for it, that gift teaches them the wrong lesson.

When we tell a child that they are special, when they misbehave, that praise teaches them the wrong lesson. When we put a child above others who worked to get where they are, that higher placement teaches them an inaccurate reflection of reality. It ruins their moral compass, and the more that compass is broken, the conscious and subconscious minds are at odds. As the conscious and subconscious separate, the chance for mental illness increases, and the individual becomes ever more troubled.

The overwhelming prevalence of narcissistic behavior can be attributed to the term "Gospel of Greed." That's why the types of mental illnesses seen in the wealthier communities are less prevalent in the poor ones, and vice versa. But make no mistake both sectors of society are mentally imbalanced to a certain extent, each in their way and for their own reasons.

These mental illnesses occur because we can't lie to our subconscious. We are experts at lying to and with the conscious; that is what being blind to our blindness is. However, the subconscious can't be lied to. Our subconscious knows who we are at our core, it will not allow us to harm others without protest. Our subconscious is preoccupied with fairness and it knows each and every time we step on others to get what we want. Our subconscious notices when we choose to harm others. It is impossible to fool our subconscious and convince it we are anything but what we truly are. Here, too, we will reap what we sow.

The more society forces us to step on other people to get ahead, the worse all our mental lives become. You might think it does not matter that you get to oppress others to get ahead, but it does, and not only to the ones being oppressed but also to the oppressor. If we keep following this "Gospel of Greed" we will eventually all become monsters, and no humans will be around to notice. As Aristotle said: "Only the good can be happy, and only the virtuous can be good."

The conscious mind tries to interpret the subconscious mind's desires/goals, since we all hate correction. When the subconscious mind desires to fix the intended behavior, guess who is there to translate that desire? The answer is the conscious mind.

It goes something like this. Imagine you're meeting

with an international businessman with a translator to translate between you both. The international visitor is irate, and they keep pointing at the translator, but you don't understand what the businessman wants. You must rely on the translator to tell you what's wrong. The businessman is telling you, "this translator is selfish, he is a thief, a murderer, he cannot be trusted, get yourself a new translator, or be ruined." The problem is "the translator" will never translate those messages. The translator will interpret "the international businessman is upset because we are not sitting outside or he wants more money on this deal." Often the translator will not tell you the truth; some call it confirmation bias or self-delusion. This device's ultimate purpose is to keep the conscious mind safe and keep internal struggle to a minimum.

This is why we are full of problems without knowing what we are or knowing the cause. The conscious mind is a sneaky bastard which will protect itself from being outed as the bad actor. as Dr Wilson puts it in "strangers to Ourselves":

> *To understand our own subconscious personality's disposition better, we cannot simply remove the veil obscuring our view, for there is no direct view, instead we are forced to make educated guesses about our subconscious' dispositions. But why don't people realize that their conscious perceptions are at odds with their subconscious personality? Does it not seem that over time people would discover that they are not the person they thought themselves to be?*
>
> *Why didn't Henry Higgins eventually realize he was not the*

refined kind-hearted gentleman who abhorred profanity? How can people be so out of touch? One reason is people are motivated to have an overly positive view of themselves and avoid looking too closely at their warts and flaws. There is a good deal of evidence that people see themselves through rose-colored glasses.

Timothy Wilson, *Strangers to Ourselves*

Yet not all avoid looking too closely:

For the good that I would I do not: but the evil which I would not, that I do. Now if I do that I would not, it is no more I that do it, but sin that dwelleth in me. I find then a law, that, when I would do good, evil is present with me. For I delight in the law of God after the inward man: But I see another law in my members, warring against the law of my mind, and bringing me into captivity to the law of sin which is in my members. O wretched man that I am! who shall deliver me from the body of this death?"

Romans 7 19-24(KJV)

The only difference between Paul and Henry Higgins is that Paul took off the rose-colored glasses and then saw the true standard and realized how far he was from it. We, in this day and age, are getting worse and worse. Instead of deciding to look honestly at ourselves, we look for more rosier-colored glasses to wear. But here again, we can't fool the subconscious. It knows how much of a monster we have turned into, for we can never make the subconscious wear those rose-colored glasses.

Mental issues are the canary in the coalmine. They

are the clearest indicator of how toxic our society has become. This free market system is constantly pressuring more and more people. We are oblivious to all the destruction it's causing as long as the Gross Domestic Product (GDP) is increasing. We lie to ourselves and say as long as the GDP is going up, eventually people will be happier. Yesterday you had a Ford and tomorrow you will get a Tesla, neither will fix our mental illnesses. When will we stop making excuses for the "Gospel of Greed"? When will we take off the rose-colored glasses and see ourselves for who we truly are? Every time we create added efficiency, it's also an added pressure on someone. The more efficiency increases the more the pressure increases on someone else.

Most of the harmful consequences of efficiency sinks to the bottom, while the majority of the beneficial results floats to the top. Humans were not meant to deal with this much pressure. All this efficiency looks good, but since fewer and fewer people are reaping the rewards, it's completely destructive to most people's mental health. Every action has an equal and opposite reaction. However, since the harmful impacts of those actions are not displayed on TV, we as a society repeat Henry Higgins actions when he looks for rose-colored glasses rather than deal with self-contradiction. Creating a world which does nothing but thinks about money will not end will.

The psychological model of thinking about money assumes that implicit reminders of money lead to self-sufficient motivation.

The priming of young children with money-related concepts or images has negatively affected their social behavior, social preferences, and psyche leading them to make more individualist and less pro-social choices and be less willing to help others. The findings suggest that the symbolic function of money is more primal than its instrumental function and that it probably develops at an earlier stage in life.

https://www.ncbi.nm.nh.gov/pmc/articles/PMC48466661

"People satisfy their needs in mainly two ways: via close communal ties or dealings with others in a market-place." (Gasiorowska et al, 2016) This type of thinking even influences the advice-giving we give each other. Thinking in a market mode will always lead us to exclude others in the pursuit of self-improvement, we must always fight that tendency, as Rev. Pauli Murray said: "When my brothers try to draw a circle to exclude me, I shall draw a larger circle to include them. Where they speak out for the privileges of a puny group, I shall shout for the rights of all mankind."

After primed with the communal mode and market mode, participants were instructed to decide whether or not give an advice (profitable or damnous) to a stranger without any feedback. The behavioral results showed that participants preferred to give the profitable advice to the stranger more slowly compared with the damnous advice, but this difference was only observed in the market mode condition ... whereas this difference was not observed at the communal mode and the control group. These findings are consistent with the dual-process system during decision-making and suggest that market mode may lead to deliberate calculation for costs and benefits when giving the profitable advice to others.

Jin, Youlong, Wei, Lei,Mei, Yu, Yipling

Here again we find the same two ideals: "do what's best for me without harming anyone" and "do what's best for others without harming anyone." It's impossible to balance the two ideals, but we constantly put the rose-colored glasses on and ignore the harm we are causing.

The over-abundance of money does not help creativity, but neither does the utter lack of resources. Most of the billionaire class came from well-to-do families, they were the only families who had access to new technology such as computers in high school. In every creative endeavor, the teacher starts with "you can make a lot of money with 'fill in the blanks,' but try not to think about money." It's known that the road to creativity is not inspired by money. At least, not at first. Money slowly becomes the primary motivator, but it hardly ever starts that way.

We have 80% to 90% of the country doing nothing but thinking about money. How much creativity do you think that kills? We will reach our maximum potential when we perform two actions: improve as much as we can and instruct others on how to improve as much as possible. In other words, learn and teach others something new. Learning and teaching not in a professional sense; instead, learning and teaching in our day to day interaction.

Why does asking someone to do a favour for you make the person being asked feel good about themselves? Why do we learn better when we teach others? It's because we are fulfilling the other part of our human responsibility. To learn is not enough, but to be truly satisfied, we need to learn and share the newly acquired knowledge with others. (And if you're like me, with hardly anyone to teach, you decide to write a book.)

Sometimes we are accepted for telling others how to improve, but most times, they reject our suggestion on how to improve. If your proposals are accepted, that's great! That's what we all want; we want everyone to improve. If others accept your ideas, you're a part of a pack. As a group you help each other improve. Get enough of you together and you help a community, then a country, and then the world. What happens if your attempts to help your friends improve are refuted?

That's when we run into all kinds of problems. When your pack rejects your attempt to improve the group, you have a few options:

> *Firstly, decide you are wrong and the pack is right, at which point you will sink to the lowest morals of the pack.*
>
> *Secondly, you can reject the pack and their moral ideas which happens far less often.*

After rejecting their ideas, that's when things get truly difficult; you will either spend a great deal of time looking for the right group or you become a loner.

This happens 10 to 30 times in life. How many of us

still talk to our first grade friends? What if we make the pack larger? Let's make the pack extremely large, like the whole world. How does that make you feel? "Overwhelmed" comes to mind. We at once feel we need to do too much for too many people and we can't possibly help them all. I suggest we think like that often. That is what it means to "love thine neighbor," all of them. We think of everyone in our family as our pack, the family is still the smallest unit in America. We like to believe individualism is our strength and it is, but Americans are not as individualistic as we imagine ourselves to be.

When we simultaneously think of ourselves as individuals and realize we are a part of a huge pack called the United States of America, or even all the people in the world, we will come up with amazing new ideas to help "the pack." For now, we know ourselves and know our pack. Being a part of such a large pack should be overwhelming. For it should urge us to greater action to help the pack. That is why religious people help each other for their pack are their fellow believers.

The left side of your brain is mainly focused on "me" and the right-side is mainly focused on "others." When we identify with a subject that others identify with, we turn the "me" into "us," that's how we form the "us" and "them" by which most view the world.

Realizing that you are a drop in the ocean is overwhelming at first, but as it sinks in, you may slowly find your hatred of others dissolve, for they are also in your pack. You will realize that your pack is not your group of friends or your family or even your place of worship, but that it's the whole earth. You will not see color or intelligence. You will not see countries or borders, or even old conflicts. You will realize the prayer of Jesus "that they may be one" John 17:21 as the idea of your connection takes hold the notion of loneliness loses its edge. The more people think of themselves as part of a whole and the more society encourages community, the less depression, anxiety and addictions we will have.

We persist in trying to cure symptoms instead of causes. We can't think of ourselves as one if we have a few ruling billionaires, even if consciously some or most don't see it. The subconscious sees it, and it's affecting us all.

The cause is always the same, not just in psychology, but politics and the economy too. The cause for all of human history has always been the same; it's always been pride. As the world adopts the American way of living (capitalism), they also slowly adopt America's psychological and social problems. The "Gospel of Greed" has serious consequences.

Most people are under so much financial pressure that it's any wonder we don't have more problems. Many comparisons are made between now and the 1920s, then also the wealth gap had reached unprecedented levels. Today, in reality, the situation is much worse. Today you get to see the wealth gap every day: on TV, on Facebook, and on Instagram. In the 1920s, Americans had their faith to give them hope and encouragement. They had healthy church communities to keep them from feeling isolated, much of that is gone in today's America.

Do we consider the issues of having each parent working and some parents working multiple jobs to support their family? Neither parents nor children have enough time in the day to learn or teach. Parents don't have time to teach their children how to be better. Both parents and children are affected negatively. Counseling and churches do help, but we need to look at where the trend is going. In "the system" Professor Reich looks at all the coping mechanisms that we have invented in the last 40 years to help us deal with the adverse effects of the "Gospel of Greed," and he points out that we are running out of coping mechanisms. We are even running out of drug coping mechanisms. Pumping millions of people full of drugs will not help society. Again, it's dealing with the symptoms, not the causes, causing far more ill than good.

So, we see that this free market capitalism destroys our mental health, dissolving our familial bonds, fracturing our social cohesion, and in time ruining our planet. Instead of letting go of the "Gospel of Greed," we press on desiring to hold onto it tighter. We must let it go and come back to the roots of what brings us fulfillment and true joy. When we have time to explore and learn and share what we have learned with our children, then the parents will feel fulfilled, and then the children will feel valued, then our world will flourish. We can't continue down the same path and expect our mental health to improve. Doing the same thing and expecting new results is after all the definition of insanity.

Every pleasureful action loses its ability to provide us

with happiness the more we repeat it. The only activities that will continuously give us new joy the more we perform it will always be helping others improve. So, the first time we purchase new shoes the purchase results in much pleasure but after the fiftieth new pairs of shoes there is hardly any happiness, each new purchase becomes more meaningless. That happens with everything only at different levels of deterioration; every repeated pleasurable action will provide you with less Dopamine than the one before it. When we help others we are rewarded differently, if we help or see others helping, we are rewarded with oxytocin, oxytocin does not diminish when you find new people to help. That's why you find doctors and pastors working till they are in their 90s. The act of helping others is the most rewarding action they can perform to give themselves joy.

SEVEN

King or Servant

BUT JESUS CALLED them unto him, and said, Ye know that the princes of the Gentiles exercise dominion over them, and they that are great exercise authority upon them. But it shall not be so among you: but whosoever will be great among you, let him be your minister; And whosoever will be chief among you, let him be your servant

Matt 22:25:27 (KJV)

Our human nature is to gather up all we can, even at others' expense; we cannot fix that innate desire ourselves. The problem now is we encourage cheating, we promote greed. The victims will not be just the ones who are economically more disadvantaged than us, but our children, whom we convince ourselves we are greedy for; they suffer now and will suffer more when the bill comes due.

With our disguised selfishness, we comfort ourselves and say "we are doing it for them." Kings also comforted themselves with the same sentiments. The ones that will pay the price of our disguised greed are those children whom we are turning from humans into cannibals. Then we wonder, why can't we help people? It is because we are incapable of thinking of others, except of ways to prey on them. I urge judges, politicians, bankers to stop, for we are going over the precipice. When we fall, it will not just be "them" that get harmed, but your children will as well. It might be that none survives this fall because we have made greed our "god" and worshipped at the altar of possession more houses, faster cars, bigger planes, stronger bombs, and larger bank accounts. Our children will die, too, because we continue to focus exclusively on the good, and we refuse to see how ugly capitalism is and always has been. It will only get uglier, and if words are not sufficient, people will find new means to express their disgust at your behavior.

We do, and should, reward the ones that create the most efficient systems, for they are constructing a better world. We want a better world; we want to speed up the process. Yet in our pursuit of a new world we must keep in mind that this new world must be for all, or it will end up being for none. How do we stop these great efficiency makers from turning around and starting the cycle of inefficiency over again? Better yet, how do we stop the abusive-rich from existing in the first place? For the abusive-rich are the leading cause of the destruction of our society with all their legal corruption. They are destroying the legitimacy of government, negating the benefit of hard work and IQ, worse of all removing any desire to love your neighbors.

Let's go back to the days of monarchs, only 300 years ago, or much less for most of the world. Let's imagine ourselves in the 1700s. We are sitting in an alehouse discussing the world and how awful it is. Of course, most people in the 1700s don't see how bad it is, since that's all they know, just like we are now not seeing the awfulness of our current environment. I say, "we need to stop having monarchs! Monarchs are an awful idea and they are the problem, not the solution!" What do you think the response of the people around me will be? The poor man will say "we have always had monarchs, our king is great, just the other day he sent everyone in the village bread, besides the devil you know is better than the devil you don't." In the other corner, a priest is eating, hearing me he responds with "God is our king and God appoints kings, it's said in Daniel 2:21 that God removes kings and establishes them do you think you are God? It also said in 1 Peter 2:13 that you should submit yourselves for the Lord's sake to every human institution, whether to a king as the one in authority. Therefore, thinking of rebelling against the king you disobey God." And in the last corner, the angriest and most afraid person, we find the prince. Now, the prince is in disguise for he does not deal with peasants, he just finds them curious. The prince says "you're talking nonsense, the king is the biggest reason you all have a home, he hires you to work in his bakery, he hires you to build his castles, he hires your children in his army. If you lose the king, you will be worse off, besides talking that way is treason and if I ever hear you repeat those words I will report you and you will be hanged."

Two hundred years later, all their children are living incredibly better lives. I propose we remove not one monarch or a few monarchs, but all born monarchs everywhere. "Every man is a king so long as he has someone to look down on" (Sinclair Lewis, *It Can't Happen Here*). I propose we remove an idea so ingrained in our minds, and I suspect I will hear these three men echoed repeatedly. Two hundred and fifty years ago, we decided that one man giving his money and power to his son was a bad idea. Today I propose that anyone giving their money and power to their children is still a bad idea.

> *When kings the sword of justice first lay down, they are no kings, though they possess the crown. Titles are shadows; crowns are empty things, the good of subjects is the end of kings.*
>
> Daniel Defoe, *The True-Born Englishman*, 1701

It took 75 years for America to make those words a reality; hopefully, we will do so again. In these days of a reincarnated monarchy, it's my sincere hope that we will find a new footing in less than 75 years and without bloodshed. The more we help our children climb the hierarchy with anything other than ideas, the worse we make it for them and the country.

Even the aristocrat's descendants are better off after

the end of monarchy, they have better medication, better homes, and higher IQs. Most importantly, they are much more likely to survive. What unimaginable advancement will we reach once we take this next step and understand that the best and fairest ways are the same? What will we be when we realise that as a people the less selfish we are, the better we will all be? Only, we can't deceive ourselves since it's easy to look at our hands and imagine them clean when they are covered with blood. Let's put the past behind us and move forward. If at any time we wish to go back to dog eat dog let us recall, the only philosophy that will ever work, "love others as yourself." It is not the monarch that hindered progress. The lack of competition was the real obstacle, and generation after generation we lower the number of genuinely competing players. We fool ourselves into thinking "three pawns" players are competing with "15 queens" players. Only those who start with a full chess set (the upper class) or with 15 queens (the billionaire class) are making money easily. For the majority of people, it's only getting ever more challenging to play this game.

It's time to stop agonizing regarding Democrats versus Republicans, or even the rich versus the poor. It's time to focus on abolishing this rigged game. We, too, love to play. We, too, love to work. We can also change the world, and I suspect we can do a much better job than many of the abusive rich. They only know how to play with 15 queens but we who suffer in myriad ways to save $1000 understand the value of money. The abusive rich buy a Rolls

Royce and lie to themselves and others by saying "I'm helping the economy," when all they are doing is helping other abusive rich.

If the child of a wealthy person starts a new company, as long as he or she started from the same line as the rest of us, and that son or daughter becomes a billionaire, we will love them. Only if they can't become a billionaire or even wealthy, then they should live as we all live, that is a free market, that is true competition. Hiring a CEO to run your parents' company while you travel the world on your private jet does not mean you are a "good chess player," it just means you started with "15 queens." Giving your inherited money to a banker or collecting rent while you do next to nothing typically means you are the abusive rich. That is just a different type of freeloader. It's not the familiar poor freeloader. The wealthy freeloader is the worst freeloader of all. Unlike the poor freeloader who is constantly told to "get a real job," no one tells these abusive freeloaders "get a real job," rather they adore them as if they did something other than get born and pampered from diaper to grave.

Getting born is not a qualification that should allow someone to rise above the rest of us. The child of the ape does not rule unless they are useful, unless they can protect as good as their parent, and unless they can provide as well as their parents. If he or she can't service any of those functions they deserve nothing. In that way, they cannot become a freeloader; before or after their parents are gone. Many saw this and came up with three systems, now the failure of all three is evident to any well-read person. In two, they kept the same selfishness, people see themselves in their children and live out the same selfishness all over again. In the third, they trusted a government to run their lives and once again we learned with great power that we eventually abuse others greatly.

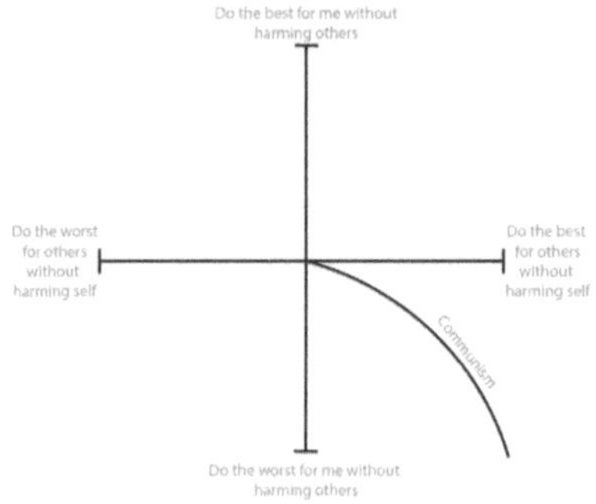

Figure 3

Communism is a theory of social and economic organization where the state owns all property and every individual contributes to the society and receives according to their needs. Communism has on several occasions, been described as a Godless, stateless, and classless society. Communism has been central in the utopian fantasies of many philosophical and even political thinkers, who have seen the mess capitalism and the "Gospel of Greed" have put humanity in. However, communism ends up where all human endeavors end, by harming more people than it helps (see Figure 4 below). Communism failed quickly compared to the system of monarchy and it did because of human greed. Or, in other words, it failed because of corruption. Greed is at the heart of all societal collapse. Common ownership is a great idea, but it does not work, because we stop working. In other words, people cheat the system but instead of 5,000,000 cheating at the top as is the case in capitalism, in communism, we have the same 5,000,000 cheats on top but we add 50,000,000 little cheats at the bottom.

Figure 4

Communistic socialism (See Figure 4 above) seems reasonable but only if you have a great deal of wealth and can perfectly balance the cheats. Such perfection does not exist; the overwhelming majority of these communistic socialistic countries fail. In most of these systems the first 30 years or so are good and later the situation starts to fall apart. There are a few examples of these countries not falling apart after a short period. These countries are typically in Europe. They have succeeded because they are the wealthiest countries in the world and have a high level of homogeneity. Slowly, it will become more challenging to support all the freeloaders as the Brexit phenomena demonstrates. Democratic socialism seems to have the answer, and currently, it's the best answer we have. However, it's only a temporary fix. With automation we are quickly approaching a place where nothing we invent will work in the future. Technology is destroying all the ways we use to structure society and that's by no means a bad thing. In times of great stress, the human spirit always adapts and creates something new and better for us all, as long as free speech is honored.

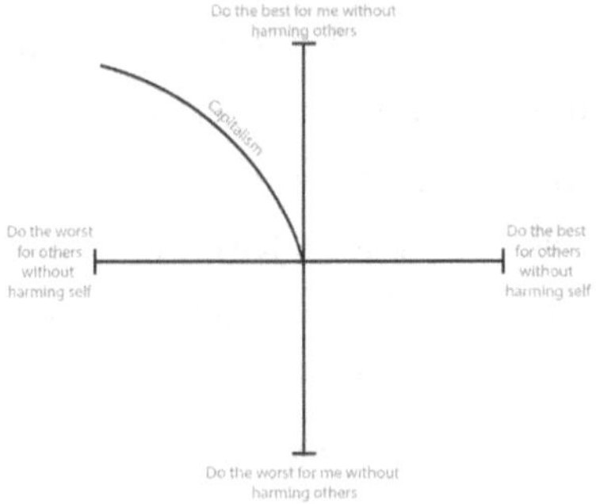

Figure 5

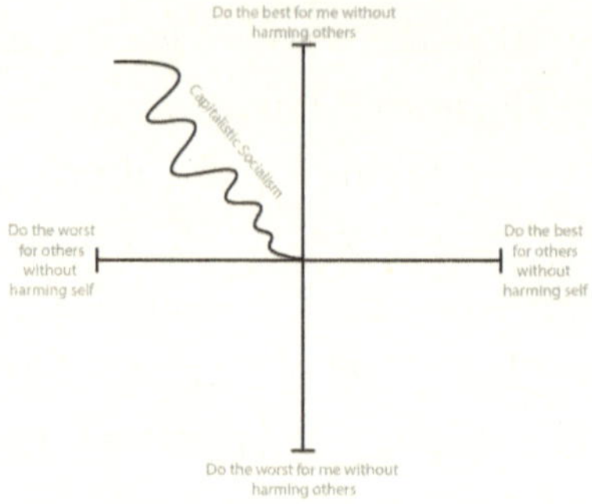

Figure 6

Capitalism (see Figure 5), or in fact capitalistic socialism (see Figure 6), was the way out and the way forward for most of the world mainly because it allows for the least number of freeloaders. Regardless, capitalism is beset with problems, and because of corruption, it's failing too, just in different ways and at a slower pace. Besides, it has a lot to answer for, as capitalism created a world divided by those who have everything and those who have nothing. It made a world where half the planet's population lives with need constantly, and a very small portion for which need is a foreign concept. Capitalism might not fail yet but it is slowly turning humans into awful creatures and it's laying the grounds for another world war. It generates a slew of other problems that are pulling us apart, as summarized in an innumerable number of books.

So instead of the great crash that was the Berlin wall

collapsing, we see the slow but inevitable giant rising. He gathers up too much wealth at the top, and when being top-heavy he falls. We call these falls the bear markets, the great recession, the great depression. They are all the result of greed. We have had three such events in only 20 years. Our solution for stopping the great giant from falling is more taxes. Let's move money from the top to the bottom, and Republicans will cry "inefficient" which is true, but how else can we keep the giant from falling? In short, I don't see the system working long and we all know this to be the case. Some systems work better than others. For example, America functions much better than China or the USSR. China has tremendous growth now but give it 30 years or less and things will turn sharply negative.

Contrary to popular opinion, China will become more despotic over time, nationally and internationally. Giving a tyrant more power does not result in a change in behavior; instead the increase in power will only serve to encourage and embolden them to continue on the same path. For now, they have learned the lesson well, "greed is good." They are ready to take greed to the next level. These will be new highs that we Americans, who have been constrained by Christianity's faint influence, never dreamed of.

For in the same breath we told the Chinese "there are no rules" and then became upset once they believed us. When China started living like there were no rules, America replied, "why are you not playing by our rules?" What awful depths will the "Gospel of Greed" take us to?

When will we wake up? Only after we are on the receiving end of such a disgusting idea do we recognize its flaws.

When we start to reap what our hands have planted in others, then we will begin to wake up. Now we come to like the "rules" only now do we dislike our harvest. We reap what we sow, we can't break that law, both domestically and internationally.

What's wrong with international politics, when Chinese-Americans or Chinese nationals steal technology? When they use what they are learning in our colleges to cheat and steal from those same colleges only then do some wake up and say "hey greed is bad, stealing is bad." The reply will inevitably be "you taught me greed was good and because of my greed I steal, therefore you taught me to be a thief." We should ask, is it only wrong now that we are the ones on the receiving end? Does it matter if the stealing is legal or illegal? (Stealing is stealing.) Stealing has never changed, but it's we who are no longer the same.

Will China wake up? The more important question before us is, will we? Just as it took me many years to understand and see what kind of monster greed had made of me, it might take generations to unlearn the "greed is good" lesson that the whole world is living out. This is the lesson that will soon destroy us all. It took 10 years of continually wondering what was wrong in me, for me to see the truth of who and what I had become. I imagine it will take some countries' generations to understand that "greed is awful." Hopefully, by the time they understand it, it's not too late for us all. With a leader who will hold the office for life, corruption is deep in the heart of the Chinese system, but the cause of the problem is always the same, human nature is always what's to blame.

When it comes to America, we have always led the way in political reformation. It falls once more on America to lead the way into a better tomorrow. Two hundred and fifty years ago, the founding fathers of this great nation pinned this singular sentence: "We hold these truths to be self-evident, that all men are created equal." That exceptional sentence has changed the course of human history many times over. It's even the most quoted sentence in the English language, and yet after 250 years we still have yet to practice what we preach. We declare that all people, all genders, are born equal. Here again, we prove we are blind to the obvious. From our beginning to this day, our pride blinds us to the obvious. The founding fathers declared three "self-evident" truths, and yet followed none of the three. While declaring "all" they had slaves, while proclaiming "men" they mistreated women, and finally, while declaring "created equal" to the king, they turned around and did the same exact thing the king did, namely create a system of inheritance. What they chastised the king for doing, they did to a lesser degree. They told the king using eloquent language "don't steal" and turned around to plot their own heist. We are experts at not recognizing our faults just the faults of others.

And why beholdest thou the mote that is in thy brother's eye, but considerest not the beam that is in thine own eye?
Matt 7:3 KJV

The founding father were great men but even in their greatest sentence they actually copied it almost word for word from St Paul who wrote:

There is neither Jew nor Greek, there is neither bond nor free, there is neither male nor female: for ye are all one in Christ Jesus.
Gal 3:28 KJV

We can't sit in judgment over the founding fathers. We should recognize that we, too, are hypocrites. We too also, don't follow our "self-evident" truth. We are all full of confirmation bias; we see what we expect to see, in others and in ourselves. This confirmation bias happens so naturally that a sentence we have quoted for 250 years does not seem to conflict with our reality and behavior. A standard of behavior is for the here and now.

Thinkest thou this to be right, that thou saidst, My righteousness is more than God's? For thou saidst, What advantage will it be unto thee? and, What profit shall I have, if I be cleansed from my sin I will answer thee, and thy companions with thee Look unto the heavens, and see; and behold the clouds which are higher than thou If thou sinnest, what doest thou against him? or if thy transgressions be multiplied, what doest thou unto him If thou be righteous, what givest thou him? or what receiveth he of thine hand? Thy wickedness may hurt a man as thou art; and thy righteousness may profit the son of man.

Job 35:2-8 KJV

We will never have perfect equality in life. Some are smarter than others and they should be rewarded for their contribution. Others work harder than the rest of us and they too should be rewarded for their effort. But in truth, the biggest difference is some win the birth lottery, or the life lottery yet the start of the race must be equal. We should not control for every variable, as the communists tried to do. But neither should we act as if the variables are totally out of our control. We must have equality of birth, for no one is born better than anyone else, nor should they ever be. It's time to declare no matter who your parents are, you will get the same opportunity to succeed as everyone else. That is our next "self-evident" truth. "All men are created equal." With those words we established the longest lasting democracy starting in 1776. With that same sentiment we fought for freedom for all in 1861. By that same weapon we took on women's inequality and Jim Crow in the 1960s. Now after 250 years of compounding inequality, it's time to fight with those same words for an equal starting line to the race of life.

It's not a problem that someone gets rich. It's not a problem that when someone creates a great company like Walmart that person becomes a billionaire. We all thank that person for making us all more efficient. But it is a problem that their children get to be born billionaires. It is a problem that they don't start on the same starting line as my children and the children of all Americans. It is a problem that that person and their children control our government through lobbying and a revolving door policy. If they make their billions in their lifetime, we love them, we salute them. But no one gets to be created above anyone else. Their kids don't become the masters of my kids just because they were born to that billionaire, just like we rejected the ruling political elites 250 years ago we now must reject the ruling economic elites.

Generational ruling economic elites are the cause of all our problems. The most prominent of which is our broken and useless political system. As we work to replace these systems of injustice, we must be cautious least in our haste to stop greed and corruption, we don't instead start greed and oppression. Too often people jump out of the frying pan and right into the fire.

After we put an end to the political elites we had three choices ahead of us: capitalism which uses laws, and innovation, and theft to keep from harming too many; communism which uses laws (often oppression), and theft to keep from harming too many; and socialism which uses laws on both the rich and the poor, and innovation, and theft to keep from harming too many. Capitalism and communism try to follow one idea or the other and the results are always a disaster. So, in effect all societies have created different degrees of socialism. We all recognize that pure communism or pure capitalism don't work. We recognized that we can't help ourselves without harming anyone and we can't help others without harming anyone. What we can do, what we must do, is let the harm happen on both sides. For all of human history, we only thought of doing one or the other, either capitalism or communism, either be a Republican or a Democrat. We will only fix this mess if we are a Republican as we live and a Democrat as we die. We will only solve this equation if we are capitalists as we live and communists when we die. Just like the law of entropy, everything we do leads to destruction. Capitalism and communism don't work because we are selfish, and worse yet, we think we are so selfless. Today, we can bring the whole world together, not by glorifying our selfishness and greed even more as Milton Freeman did, but by fighting against our selfishness. Glorifying selfishness will lead to wars and will never lead to unity. Glorifying greed will lead to hatred and not love. Only once we see how ugly we truly are and realize how far from "love my neighbor as myself" we have drifted.

Then we can start back on the right path. Once we admit we are all greedy, then we can look at how we get everyone to confront their own greed and to try and fight it in their own life. It's just another human bug we have to deal with. In the eighteenth century, Adam Smith dealt with it to the best of his abilities given the time in which he lived, and Christianity largely restrained cannibalistic capitalism. Thanks to technology our toolbox is much larger now. Our ability to hold people accountable is much easier. We must use our technology to fight against greed, instead of continuing to use all this technology to enable greed to expand ever more, granting our greed free reign will end horribly for all involved.

The new way will neither be capitalist or communist. For once we recognize our flaws and our overt and disguised selfishness. Only then can we understand how to meet both ideals. Once we realize that the two ideals can never be combined, then we realize the answer to one of the most difficult questions in history. A question which despite our super computers, our high-level math, our supposed great advancement has eluded us for generations. The answer is not "greed is good," neither is sacrifice good. Since we can never advance without harming anyone, and we can never help others without harming anyone, the answer is we must do both. We concede that we will harm, but we must end the harm after only one generation. Just as walking is a forward motion through falling, the way to a better future will only come through sacrifice after greed. We must create a cycle of continually redistributing all wealth so that we can start a new generation of "true competitors." We keep differentiating at birth and we keep creating abusive rich which do greater harm than good. As a society, we must concede that advancement requires losers but we also must acknowledge born winners we will not abide. The problem is we created a system that can never survive inherited wealth, nor should it. Creating a system of oppression and calling it competition will no longer fool anyone. There isn't a better system than capitalism. The only problem is that we keep adding inherited wealth, which when added destroys any hope of a better tomorrow for the overwhelming majority of humanity as we blind ourselves and say they need to compete and compete. Compete with what? It's similar to sending farmers against a fully equipped army and calling it a war, no matter how much some try to call it a war, it's nothing more than genocide.

Just as we thought ruling families should not inherit the country, it's time to realize no one should inherit anything. As is always the case, our biggest flaw is only seeing the fault of others, not ourselves. When in the 1700s most of our families were peasants, our ancestors looked at the aristocracy with envy and hate, not only for how they were treating them, but also, they wanted to be them. Never mind that being them covered their hands with blood. We would have been better if we were all peasants not giving our children our possessions. However, selfishness takes on many forms, and seeing our disguised selfishness takes many generations. Once we are all peasants, we all inherit everything, we all inherit the good just as we all inherit the bad. We all work for the good just as we all suffer the ill. In that way, we all can keep each other accountable. That way we can find the cannibals easily and reward the useful ones quicker. That way we stop competing about who will destroy the human race first. We have been doing that for a long time and someone is bound to win that disastrous game. If we wish to survive as a country and as a world, we must live up to our self-evident truth.

I am not bound to win, but I am bound to be true. I am not bound to succeed, but I am bound to live by the light that I have. I must stand with anybody that stands right, and stand with him while he is right, and part with him when he goes wrong.

Abraham Lincoln

EIGHT

Government or Community

THE PERPETUAL OWNERSHIP of capital by a person as in monarchy, a government as in communism, or a social class as in capitalism is wrong and harmful and destined to fail. Whatever you want from your society ending all personal inheritance and replacing it with national inheritance will deliver it:

- If you desire a small efficient government, end all inheritance, and have the government collect fewer taxes, and raise money by auctioning the goods of those who die. More on that in the next chapter.
- If you desire a meritocratic society, end all inheritance and that way our higher education will not be ever more filled with the rich and not the intelligent.
- If you want true healthy competition, you will

end all inheritance so everyone will be able to "truly compete" starting on the same line.

- If you want justice in the judicial system, end all inheritance, that way all will be genuinely equal before the law instead of the rich receiving special treatment.
- If you want safety, end all inheritance, and crime will practically disappear for most crimes are out of necessity or resentment and not much else.
- If you want true democracy, end all inheritance and each person will be heard instead of the billionaire class controlling our government.
- If you want more freedom, end all inheritance and you will have many more hours in the day to follow your interest instead of working 50 or 60 hours a week.
- If you want to educate people, end all inheritance everyone will more time to learn and grow if you want to be ready for the next disaster,
- End all inheritance and people will be able to truly see the problems coming instead of always having an eye on money.
- End all inheritance and 80% of all corruption will end. There will be too many eyes looking out for all our good instead of just the police.
- End all inheritance if you don't want to live in a dystopia in 50 to 100 years' time, for by then

the voice of the people will mean nothing, it almost already doesn't.
- End all inheritance if you don't want self-annihilation 150 to 200 years from now, for sooner or later the injustice will be met with violence nationally or internationally.
- Ending all inheritance will improve the lives of 90% of the country and for the last 10% of people, their grandchildren's lives will also be improved, exactly similar to what happened when we ended the monarchy from having its inheritance.

Apportioning inheritances should be a crime, the worst crime of all. But we let all do it, just like slavery was an unrecognized crime for generations. Inheritance is this generation's unrecognized crime. Only, it's a crime against billions of people, not just against millions of black people.

If and when the human race comes to an end, we will meet our end at the hands of the "Gospel of Greed." Hopefully, we will wake up before that day arrives. There has never been a difference between greed and pride. Greed is just the outcome of pride. Why do I deserve more than others? Because I am better than others.

There are many ways to govern a country, but there is only one way that can last. The only right way I know is ingrained in the command "love your neighbors as ourselves." Just as an angle has an infinite number of degrees, yet only one can be a 90-degree angle. There are an infinite number of wrong ways and only one right way that can get us to truly live up to "love thy neighbors as ourselves." Selling more debt to the rich will not work, monetizing more debt will not work, and closing more tax loopholes will not work.

None of our "fixes" will work if we keep inheritances. Our economies and societies will worsen, similar to Europe's monarchs who genuinely wished to fix their countries problems, but also wanted to remain in power. We have new monarchs who wish to improve the country on one condition, that condition is they remain as the perpetual elite.

If we want a better world, we must be willing to sacrifice for that better world. The choice is either a better world or we keep our monarchs. Just like we stopped the political elites from getting an inheritance 250 years ago, we must do the same now. We have many who desire to create a better world, but also who want to continue to be the monarchs of that better world. The reality is those two goals are mutually exclusive. The better world always has more rulers and the fewer the monarchs there are, the less they wish to share power. For neither pride nor greed has any interest in sharing.

We can hardly blame the founding fathers, for in their time they were some of the fairest and most conscientious people in existence. Now and then we had to improve upon their work, and it's time to do so again. The "better world" always has more monarchs than the one before it. As the concentration of wealth increases, we destroy ourselves. Countries that lose their internal cohesion will fail in due time, and nothing is more destructive to internal cohesion than ever growing numbers of billionaires and the growing number of homeless. As we join the rest of the world in having a ruling class, we join the rest of the world as being another oppressive country, slowly turning into a dystopia. As more freedom is relinquished in the name of security or in the desire for a safety net, they both must be rejected. The abuse of power will never stop whether it's political or economic. It has gotten to a point that the two abusers rely on each other, instead of the government being for the people by the people. In time the government becomes a government for the rich by the rich. If this trend is not stopped from spiraling out of control now, governments will turn on the people for the benefit and protection of corporations. As the wealthy becomes the main funders of governments, these governments become more beholden to corporations. Again, we enter an echo chamber of both growing and relying on each other to grow, leaving the average citizen behind. As it continues citizens will feel increasingly powerless to affect change. The only solution is to state, whatever benefits a person gets at birth, those benefits must be given to all. We can't be allowed to cheat and start ahead of others.

Republicans are right, we need competition, we need a free market, but there is no competition between a player who starts with three pawns and another who starts with 15 queens. Just like there was no competition between the prince and the baker's son. We can't achieve a better world while holding on tightly to power, such an attitude has never worked and is doomed to end in conflict. Just like democracy and monarchy never coexisted, democracy and oligarchy will never coexist. We wonder what people see in China or why the Chinese don't want our system. The answer is they see what has become of the other countries who followed our way. Most Americans constantly rail against democracy and voting and the two-party system when in reality it's capitalism that is our enemy, not democracy. Only we love our greed, it is our beloved pet, we dare not harm it, rather we keep feeding it and giving it all it demands and it's getting ready to swallow us whole.

While we may all feel that a classless society wouldn't be all that bad, we need to remember that the effective and proven pillars of this economic system revolve around the antithesis of everything that has made America the greatest nation on earth. This is why for every socialist state in modern history there has always been a corresponding dictator figure, lording the affairs of the state and crushing every resistance. As for Europe's communistic socialism their story is yet to be fully told.

Even though socialism always tries to rebrand itself, it is imperative not to forget that dictatorship and centralized control are the functioning bases of this system. In every socialist state you will always see an individual or a select group whose motive is to stay in power for as long as possible and this mandate is usually defended by any means possible including incarceration forced sterilization and organ harvesting often murder. The ability to change the laws of the country and direct its economy allows the dictators to restrict freedom of speech and movement, vanquish any opposition, kill innocent persons as "scape-goats," and isolate the citizens from the rest of the world. All to avoid the most feared outcome of losing their hold on power.

Money and power are two sides of the same coin. Neither should be held in the hands of the few. It does not matter if those few are the few in politics or the few in business. Humans will abuse their power regardless of how they got it and who they were before they got such power, that's why oversight is imperative. When money, and consequently power, is given to a very wide base the whole country becomes stronger, that's what this new system will do, once again create the largest middle class in the world.

NINE

Economics or Ethics

FINALLY, we come to the heart of the matter. Now, we come face to face with our greed and how for 300 years we have been weaponizing money. From the days of Adam Smith till now we have been perfecting this weaponization. Money is now a weapon of mass destruction against the poor and our society, and yet we wring our hands at the destruction our choices are causing. How has the wealth gap become so large? Why can't people close the wealth gap? Worse yet, why is the situation digressing despite all our effort? The Gini Index is a numerical representation of the income difference between the rich and the poor in the same country. It is a numerical representation of how revolting a society has become. If the coefficient is 0, then we achieve absolute equality, if the coefficient is 1, then we degenerate to absolute inequality (see Figure 7 below).

Figure 7

1. The Gini Coefficient has been steadily increasing since 1969, a period in which the U.S. economy has experienced dramatic and comparatively consistent economic growth. Note that the post WW-II period of economic recession (1948–1958) is the only period in which the Gini Coefficient declined significantly in recent history. 2. Note that the Gini coefficient began its most rapid increase beginning about 1981, which coincides with the widespread use of computers.

We have been building weapons of mass destruction for the rich and against the poor for close to 50 years. Examples of these weapons include credit default swaps, derivative swaps, stock buyback, options, hedge funds, trading algorithms. Our greed's harmful consequences accumulate; meanwhile our response grows more oblivious. Once we see how ugly this system is, it's impossible to unsee, just like long ago people saw how ugly slavery was, and it was impossible to unsee. Changing this "Gospel of Greed" is the challenge of our time and if we fail, there might not be another chance to get it right.

As a result of capitalism, most have become ever

more monster-like, and monsters avoid mirrors. Even if they happen to pass a mirror by, they will only focus on the attractive parts to appease their conscience, ignoring the overwhelming ugliness. I refuse to take part in this modern-day "structural genocide" any longer. Suppose you feel that only communism or socialism has destroyed lives and capitalism on the other hand has been great, the only justification for thinking capitalism is great, stems from confirmation bias. In other words, confirmation bias is supporting what you already believe, approving of a monopoly game in which you start with 1000 times more than others is no surprise. Capitalism did not kill its own people, it kills others and has murdered those in other countries, and now it's doing internally what it did externally for decades. For the last 50 years, capitalism has turned to devouring itself, the infamous snake eating its tail. Once Wall street devours Main Street completely it will then starve, and once it's dying of starvation, we will have another war. There is no way to stop the cycle quickly, but we must start to change this system. If we continue to be oblivious to our awfulness, there will be unimaginable consequences. Capitalism is a runaway train that crushes the weaker: billions of lives down the line with every new bear market and recession or even depression. We have desensitized ourselves to the harm we cause. Genocide is everywhere and we hardly mind no the gini coefficince for the world is at an all-time high. Unlike the Nazis who had someone to stop them, no one's left to stop this insanity. We have utterly forsaken any responsibility to the average person long ago. We are most definitely not a city on a hill anymore, and we have not been for a long time.

Except for a small number of leaders, most are happily driving us to our destruction. Every time the road ahead looks worse than the road we are leaving behind, economists, bankers, and politicians assure us "the car will work, this time." They speak of compounding interest but ignore the fact that in truth it's compounding misery and destruction. They tell of its magic in reality, it's a mirage of compounding, new companies don't add market capitalization from thin air. The virtue of a free market is full of vice. All the stock market amounts to is a situation where one company rises while many others fall (with the exception of pharmaceutical or medical stocks), we just shift money from one place to another. We moved so much wealth to the top and now after we surpassed the greatest level of inequality in our history, we continue wringing our hands in dismay at our own work. This cruelty did not happen fluidly. Instead, it is the premeditated action of a group of people who in their self-delusion drive the world to wars, all in the name of that awful game of "the one who dies with the most toys wins." And again, we must learn that ends don't justify the means. Worse yet, wrong behavior always culminates in awful results. It seems we are determined in repeating the mistakes of the past. Chang puts it well in his book *The Bad Samaritans*:

> *The poor growth record of neoliberal globalization since the 1980s is particularly embarrassing. Accelerating growth – if*

necessary at the cost of increasing inequality and possibly some increase in poverty – was the proclaimed goal of neoliberal reform. We have been repeatedly told that we first have to 'create more wealth' before we can distribute it more widely and that neoliberalism was the way to do that. As a result of neoliberal policies, income inequality has increased in most countries as predicted, but growth has actually slowed down significantly. Moreover, economic instability has seen a marked increase during the period of neoliberal dominance. The world, especially the developing world, has seen more frequent and larger-scale financial crises since the 1980s. In other words, neoliberal globalization has failed to deliver on all fronts of economic life: growth, equality, and stability. Despite this, we are constantly told how neoliberal globalization has brought unprecedented benefits. The distortion of facts in the official history of globalization is evident at the country level. Contrary to what the orthodoxy would have us believe, virtually all the successful developing countries since the World War II initially succeeded through nationalistic policies, using protection, subsidies, and other forms of government intervention.

H. Chang, *The Bad Samaritans*

Capitalism is a system that continually presses the weaker until they have nothing more to give. The weak now constitute 90% of all of us. When will we wake up? Will we wake up when the weak reach 99% of the total or maybe when it reaches 99.99%? If 90% of Americans can't affect change, when will we be able to? We can't look to others to do it for us, for they harm hundreds of millions, and pat themselves on the back because tens of thousands were enriched.

Wall Street has been selling America to buy China for 50 years, as long as they can make an extra dollar, Wall Street will do whatever it takes to make that money, no matter the consequences. We regularly fool ourselves with the stock market as if these companies and their consistent growth come from nowhere. That 8% growth is 8% of added pressure on someone, either the employees, other companies or countries, or the planet. Someone is getting harmed for someone else's stock to rise; many are getting ever more depressed for someone to buy another Rolex. Many can't buy diapers as a result of a few being able to buy a second vacation home. That upward trend has an end, and its future might be the end of us all. Still, we wonder, where did we go wrong?

Recently, I saw a picture that perfectly exemplifies the insanity we are living. In this picture, which was on Cramer's *Mad Money.* In the one corner the text "best week for stocks since 1938," appears. Text at the bottom of the picture states that more than 16 million Americans have lost their jobs in three weeks. This picture is attached to an article with the question "Why stocks rally when things are terrible?" We might as well ask "why cannibals are full ... in a famine?" We wonder why can't we come up with a better system? The answer is easy, we have gotten used to a diet of human flesh and don't intend to give it up.

The only current way to turn the cannibals into humans again is through taxes. This just repeats what the monarchs of the past did to us. Such actions will not stop the cannibals. it's only turning us more into cannibals. Taxes only delay the inevitable. Taxes take some of the money that has flowed to the top producers/abusers and distributes it to the bottom again (albeit inefficiently). In other words, we take money from Jeff Bezos and give it to people in the form of food stamps and/or Medicaid. Some might want to add salaries in this system, but wages don't count.

First, we must acknowledge that no employer hires any worker out of kindness or generosity; they only hire out of necessity and self-interest. If an employer's total pay including taxes and benefits is $15 an hour per employee, that employer must make at least $15.01. Typically, an employer makes double what the employee makes, so if an employee is paid $15 an hour, the employer usually needs to make $30 an hour from the employee's work. Now, some might say, "They choose to give their time for that amount of money. No one forced them to work for only $15 an hour." Regardless of choice or requirement neither eliminate the imbalance of power between the employee and the employers. A conman cheats by creating a false world and the mark chooses to part with their money. Does this mean the conman is a good guy since the victim decides to part with their money? We again fall in the same trap. We humans are all too willing to accept, or ignore the harm, as long as it's not too extreme. The conman and the employer are different but only in degree but not in kind. If I must get more profit out of a worker than what I pay the employee in wages, then it does not matter how much I pay them, for the employer will always make more than the employees. The only company paying their employees more than they are getting out of them in profit is a soon to be a bankrupt company. That is the nature of cheating. It can't be changed. However, just because it can't be fixed does not mean it should not be acknowledged.

The traditional way to solve this problem in America is to raise the minimum wage. This only fixes the symptom, not the cause of the problem. If we succeed in making the minimum wage $15 an hour, it changes nothing for the employer who will still have to get more out of the worker than they pay them to stay in business. If we raise the minimum wage to $50 an hour, after some time we will run against the same problem. We keep pushing contradictory views down the road, not recognizing that the problem is us. Now, we are running out of road to brush the problems onto. Now we have an outraged citizenry that will continue to worsen until we can't deal with them because we refuse to see the truth. Capitalism is a flawed system, the same as socialism and communism. All three are failures, and all create a cruel existence.

We keep kicking the can down the road, we have a name for this problem of delaying ideology, it's called inflation. Inflation is the taskmaster we would rather have than the alternative. Its cousin, deflation, is crueler. Inflation is the small rift between our income and the price of goods that become a chasm that most can't cross over time. Having family in Egypt, I have seen inflation play out very harshly. The Egyptian pound value went from 1 pound equaling $0.13 in October 2016 to 1 pound equaling $0.06 in November 2016. If the significance of that change is not clear, here is an example to help: if I wanted to buy a car that was worth $20,000 in October but did not, in November, that car would cost $40,000. My intention is not to make you feel sorry for Egypt or Egyptians (for whom my heart breaks) but to understand the system and its effect on the whole world, this same scenario happened in Turkey and England and many other countries. The current economic model is unsustainable and will always lead to economic oppression and collapse. Our leaders in the devolved world know this, so to "fix" the system, they have added another bandage: central banks. The central banks are our best effort to keep inflation stable. They attempt to hold inflation at or around 2%. As I write, many are sitting right now discussing how to keep things from falling apart at the start of what I suspect will be the Covid-19 recession, if not depression. I'm sure they will talk about many things that I don't understand. I'm sure they will have many mathematical models showing different ways to fix the problems we are facing, and ways to prop up this system. I'm also sure no one will look at the cause. All they will see, and discuss, is the patient's symptoms. The worst part of human nature is the cause. Greed is always the cause for that is what makes a person attempt to take advantage of another.

An economy requires people who can afford the goods and services that are being made. If there are

100,000 inventors, but only 5% of the population that can afford their inventions, we will not have an economy. Americans have understood this implicitly in the past through Christianity. Now as a result of the "death of God" we ran amok of Adam Smith's greed. He simply underestimated the greed we were truly capable of, for people were constrained by their conscience much more in 1720 than they are in 2020. A case in point was Henry Ford, who paid his employees so much more than the average to the extent that other rich people disapproved of his Christian ways. Other business leaders at the time told Ford "you can pay your employees a lot less." In other words, "you need to cheat better than that." They were telling him that he was making the rest of the oligarchy look bad. He answered, "only people who make good money can afford to buy my cars." Often, efficiency starts with the best of intentions, First-generation rich see a need and fill that gap; they are typically high in conscientiousness. The problem intensifies with the next generation who turn from mostly useful rich to mostly abusive-full rich. Second generation rich, often don't see a need, they only see a profit margin. What do you do to compete? You start abusing the system even more to stay on top.

The days of monarchs are long past us, but we have created new rulers, crueler kings, leaders who feel no responsibility for the havoc they are causing; since they go from their private jets to their private islands and think themselves angels. One of the most disturbing books I ever read was *Homo Deus* by Yuval Harari. Forget Stephen king, if you wish to be genuinely terrified, read that book. *Homo Deus* was scary, not because I disagreed with Harari but instead because I wholeheartedly agreed with him.

A technological revolution without a moral revolution is the waking nightmare we are in and it will only get worse. With all due respect to Harari, he thinks we are turning into gods, and I must disagree. If we wish to advance, we must foster morality first, for the more we ramp up technology without elevating morals the easier the well positioned will take advantage of the rest. The more technology lets us do, the more it will allow the few to control the masses. If those few are monsters without knowing it, the more we will all suffer. We only need to look at all of human history to realize that every advancement to date has been first and foremost used for oppression. Now, after 50 years of technological advancement, what do we have in America? We have only the most economically oppressed American citizens in the history of our country. It's time to stop thinking we are becoming gods, for all statistical and measurable evidence are unquestionable, pointing in precisely the opposite direction.

All evidence shows we are drifting far from the ideal world that we created in *Star Trek* and the like. Instead, we are headed into a world that looks precisely the opposite direction. It's time to take off the rose-colored glasses, no matter how rosy we make them, they will not help. We have stopped focusing on moral advancement and that is what's needed much more than technological advancement. Moral improvements are how we evolve into something better. Instead. Because of our inattentional blindness to morality we are headed into a world where once again the few rule over the many. However, this time it is happening with ruthless efficiency, and with the efficiency of technology. We can see hints of it starting in China where every citizen is watched 24/7 and given a social credit score. We can't allow our world to turn back the time to 500 years ago. We must change, and the only change is to give more people power and eliminate the concentration of power (political or economic) in the hands of a few. If the last 50 years have taught us anything, it's that money is more powerful than governments. However, it's not yet more indomitable than "we the people" or the human spirit. Now is our time to put a stop to this insanity.

We have to come to a place where we view money in terms of people's lives. If you improve our lives in return, you get some of our lives given to you. That is what money does in a free capitalist society. Someone was harmed for you to make money, it doesn't come from nothing, no matter what tricks we try to use. It is a zero-sum game. The only lag in the game is it takes decades to balance the books. Similar to not accepting blood diamonds from Africa, no one should want to inherit money, for all money is blood money. Each of us needs to make our own money by helping the people in our lives, with our own abilities, then we will get rewarded with others' lives

Some might ask: Why has America succeeded for so long at giving opportunities to so many? How has it grown so fast? The answer is similar to the reason Germany and Japan did well in their transformation. It is the same reason we see China grow now. Growth is happening because they were developing countries, but more crucially, they had a real race. They had a race where the majority started on the same line. The United States lasted as a country of opportunity for so many because of precisely what this book proposes: citizens starting at the same point. Immigrants came from all corners of the world and they all started at the same level as each other. They came with virtually nothing and had to make their way in a new country. As one state got filled, people started with nothing in a new state. However, that generation died in the 1920s. From the 1900s we began to have increasingly more citizens start their lives with more than others. Then slowly they had children who began with even more; the cycle of capitalism continues and the patient we call the American dream died. We elect one "doctor" after another, intending to revive the patient only for the deterioration to accelerate. Our country becomes more divided and the rest of the world races to become another America. Until we elect a mortician, instead of a doctor, one who will make us feel good about our dying dream. A mortician dresses up the dead man and makes him sing and dance, but in reality, the patient is long dead. Can we raise our dead dream again? Maybe, but we can't do it by living in a fantasy or giving the patient the illusion of life. We must start by freely admitting, the dream is dead and we are its murderers. Our greed killed it; our blindness killed it. But if we act, and if we act boldly and decisively, we can bring back the dream that is America and heal the people that I love.

We can't fix the system with more taxes. Taxing wealth will help but it will just be another bandage to try and cure the cancer that is greed. The only economic way forward is to have an equal starting line. Once people have accumulated all the wealth on the top, we must thank them for they made us extremely efficient. However, their children should not get any of their wealth, being the child of the rich is enough of a leg up on the rest of the country. If they can't do well for themselves with that amount of an advantage over the rest, they have no right to stay at the top. In that way, we will have a true ecosystem, not dissimilar to the one we all learn about as children. Water slowly evaporates over many months and is quickly released to start a new life. If we have water that goes up only, we will be left with a desert sooner or later. Once all our accumulated wealth goes not only to our children but also to all of our children, we will all live in a new world. If we continue down this path, we will find self-destruction meeting the whole world.

Money needs to flow from the old to the young and not from the rich to the poor. Some might argue as my dear mother asked "why would people work if they can't leave their money to their kids?" My answer to her and anyone who asks, I don't have a child and I'm working plenty. Wanting to have a better life is why we work, not necessarily for our children. Remember, we are all selfish.

Acting in one's self-interest doesn't need to be encouraged, we are looking out for number one from the day we are born to the day we die. Instead of encouraging greed, let's encourage acting in the interest of others. We can strive to improve the lives of all the children of America, indirectly enhancing our children's lives. We can work to teach all children and make them productive people in society.

In many cases, an inheritance is used as an excuse to ignore our children. Besides, a big part of all familial infighting occurs because of inheritance. Even more disturbing is the fact that inheritance and life insurance policies are the major cause of most murders. How much better will the world be if all that is eliminated? Let us work for the good of our children as well as our neighbor's children. We can give our children a better and more equal world. We can provide our children with a cleaner and longer lasting world. Once we realize that the cause of our problems is not each other, something positive is achievable. It's not the ones who make too much or the ones who make too little that are the issue, but the problem is in our nature. After admitting our true nature then we can begin to solve the actual cause of all these systemic problems. We can stop arguing about symptoms and move onto curing the ultimate cancer that is selfishness and greed.

From the time we are born to the day we die we repeat one word. Right after we learn the words "mommy" and "daddy" we are experts at "mine": my toy, my car, my house, my money. Long after we stop saying mommy and daddy, we continue to say "mine" till the day we die, even after we die, from the grave we shout to the world one last time "mine." To some the mirror of death is impossible to ignore; they decide it's time to change, however, even such a revelation seldom occurs. We can't rely on the desire of a few for self-correction, for that only leaves us the worst kinds of people, the ones on whom mirrors are ineffectual. Those thanks to technology, are growing more dominant generation after generation as they grow, they are strangling society, democracy, and our planet. From the cradle to the grave, greed has us in its clutches. For the child, the answer is simply to force them to let go of their toys. What shall we say to the adult? We must tell them the same thing, for human nature does not change; it just finds new ways to hide its ugliness. We, the people, must give the adults the same instructions as the parents order their children. We say to them, you "must let go." We let them have our toys while they were alive, but their children don't get to keep our toys once they have gone. Their toys will be auctioned, all of them, for they only borrowed our money. We the people, played with them, for they made us better, but our money is still our money. With our newly relinquished money, we will vote for a new efficiency maker who will make us all even better.

This is how we reach this great world full of inventions and progress, not by greed but by cooperation, not by doing what's best for the self but by starting with what is best for others, not by monarchs who appoint their children as our princes to rule over us, but by having a clean race, a fair race. The more unfair and lopsided race is, the less useful markets are. And our markets have become very unfair; hence it's become useless in creating a better world for the over-whelming majority of Americans.

You will recall a question from the start of this book in Chapter 1 which I did not answer concerning the investor who buys a house, fixes it, and expects to make money from his labor. I agree completely that if you create efficiency, you should be rewarded. I also agree that we vote on who has done a better job by giving him or her our money, that is the function of a market and it's a great system. Our market is much more abusive than free now. Capitalism requires most of the available money to flow upward to the top to the useful and abusive rich the owners of capital. Fine, but the money can't stay at the top indefinitely. Some even call this the middle-class trap. It's most definitely not the middle classes' fault that we find ourselves in this situation, but we love to wear those rose-colored glasses, or worse yet, it's an intentional misdirection on the part of some. In either case, it's wrong. In *Capital* by Thomas Piketty we learn that we've been playing this game for 300 years. Piketty states that our actual progress, accounting for population and inflation, is close to 1% a year for 300 years, which is wholly insufficient in this day and age.

We slowly move money from one wealthy family to another rich family, creating little actual progress. We slowly move money from one rich landlord to another rich landlord until someday we will all turn into renters. We are a generation of surfs, as Steve Bannon describes us. Now according to new research for the first time since the Great Depression, the majority of young adults in the United States now live with their parents. I'm not sure what is required to wake us up if statistics that equate our time to the Great Depression is not doing the trick. Bannon does not give much of an answer to this generation of surfs or to the ones to follow who will only live worse lives. Bannon correctly identifies a problem, but like many that came before him, he does not pinpoint the right cause nor any kind of solution.

Let's imagine ourselves as Dr. House. We know that the patient we call the "American Dream" is in bad shape. We know if we don't do something, he might die, which is better than giving him nothing or giving the patient the wrong medicine. Either way, the patient will die. If we keep giving our economy the wrong cures, the patient will die. If we do nothing, the results will be the same. Inevitably we will find ourselves in the current situation trying to figure out how to bring some of the money that flowed to the top producers/abusers down again. Traditionally, that was achieved with taxes, and to varying success. If we stop acting immoral, then maybe we can get out of this before we truly reap what we sow. On that day, there will be no more chances. Every action has an equal and opposite reaction. If millions of Americans have nothing, then they will have nothing to protect and nothing to bind them to each other and our country, then where will we end up?

I can't hope to write about how we can change every detail of society after we eliminate inheritance in just one book; neither would most want to read it. However, here are presented few ideas on how we can achieve this new world. These are just a blueprint and are not meant as absolutes.

Inherited capital and inherited real estate are the problems of capitalism. Without eliminating them, capitalism will only worsen, till we are all living in a dystopia worse than ever before. This new system will have a 50 years transitional period if done peacefully.

- Instead of taxing income, the government gets its money from auctioning off all the possessions of those who died. Government auctions are to US-born citizens only. Obtaining citizenship by birthing visa holders and through buying passports can't continue.
- Since corporations are now considered as people, they will be the only persons able to inherit any wealth.
- Access to our market requires that other countries change their system to one that does not include inheritance, similar to what we will have done with capitalism and free markets.
- Bidding on relinquished positions is restricted to a person's net wealth so that, if the value of a house is $50,000 that person can't bid on it if their net worth is higher than $100,000 (that way equal players compete).
- Stocks are already liquid and can easily be combined to give each new-born 1000 S&P.

Alternatively, we can create a whole new US stock that can be traded just like the Russell 2000 or the S&P or an ETF. People can access their money when they graduate from college or when they turn 21.

- No corporations can own private real estate, for they never die.
- Private corporations or private businesses are the most difficult element to tackle, but like real estate, they can also be auctioned off or the new inheritors can pay back a loan of the value of the company over 10 or 15 years. Massive private companies can be turned into public companies or be auctioned off into smaller businesses.
- To limit the transfer of wealth to relatives a person can only pay their relatives the average salary of such a position nationally. For example, if the average Vice-President at a similar job gets $300,000, then the son or daughter can only get approximately $300,000 max. People will try to cheat, but just like cheating on their taxes the new cheating will be inheritance cheating; it will be the new ongoing battle of governments and corporations.
- The best thing a parent can leave a child is a good, well-managed company, a business that his or her children can manage, use to pay for their education, give them all they want so that

they can succeed without giving them anything they can use to lord over others. So, parents can only give gifts that will decrease in value such as cars and boats, and even those must have a low limit.

- To keep the playing field equal, the government can only give three or four newborns of each family the "national inheritance." If a family has more kids, then they can leave their kids the same amount as all the rest (equal starting line) as a society we can only help three or four children max per couple that will have to be calculated mathematically (remember we are all cheats and we can't let some cheat by having an exorbitant number of kids).
- By ending all inheritance, we turn the house from an appreciating commodity into a depreciating commodity like cars, and we limit the rich from playing the real estate game easily by listing bidders by their net wealth, since the 15 queens player love to challenge the three pawn players as they know they will always win. Real estate is far too easy of a game for the rich to win and it's all a useless and harmful game for society, it helps a few and harms billions.
- As for real estate development projects, they will require cooperation and not domination, the developer will need to work out a deal with

> the current owner if, let's say, 70% agree then the project can go on. Or of course they can use normal market forces such as buying the houses from their current owners as is the case now.

If money is transferable from one generation to another, corporations will be incentivized to be more responsible, rather than needing the taxpayer to constantly bail them out, since they are too big to fail. when taxpayers are required to shield the rich from the consequences of their actions (that system is no longer capitalism). America has created a class of elite for whom their well-being and the country's well-being are at odds. So, in order to build themselves up, they tear America down. Just as the spoiled child who is shielded from the consequences of their actions by his parents, they will eventually become an awful adult. We have created lots of awful corporations. The founders and executive suite have learned to create failed corporations in order to enrich themselves and their families. And when it all comes crashing down, they declare bankruptcy, absolving themselves of all responsibilities passing the bill to lenders or the government. Chief abuser of that system is our current president who was rewarded with the most honorable position in America for doing the most dishonorable acts (teaching millions the worst lesson possible). Once there is no inheritance, if one creates a company that can last, you can leave the company's management to your children, which will give them quite a leg up, but it will also force you to create a lasting company. Capitalism, where billionaires win when they create a business is great, but capitalism in which billionaires win when their business goes bankrupt is not capitalism. This is crony capitalism, in which America elites privatize profits and turn losses over to the public sector. It's a system of rewarding the incompetent and the dishonest, and no country will last long by rewarding incompetence and cheats, not even America.

Crony capitalism is now part and parcel of our economic system. Through the revolving door between the corporations and Washington D.C., each side knows they have a friend on the other side. The reality is we are no longer capitalist or socialist, or even communist. Our system has turned into a crony capitalist system where the political elite shield the economic elite from the consequences of their harmful actions. The shield is employed by the political elites and is the sweat and lives of the middle and lower working classes. When the US government holds up the whole market, with 4 trillion in credit and loans again to shield all these companies from the consequences of their actions, all it's doing is making things worse for the next time, five years from now $4 trillion will not be enough. Corporate America will require $8 trillion. Over and over making fewer and fewer extremely wealthy and crushing 80% of the United States population. It's time we recognize that this no longer works, it had its time but its time is over. Once a system harms more people than it helps, then it's time to admit intentions don't matter, only results matter. The fact that the system has lasted for 300 years implies that it is much better than other systems, socialism or communism, but it's time to say goodbye. Capitalism has got us to where we are, but for 50 years it has been making the situation worse for society and 50 years of degradation is long enough.

Some may feel the new system would inhibit growth and innovation. In reality, it's the current system which has inhibited growth since it greatly limits competition. Firstly, it will help create much stronger bonds in communities and schools. Secondly, it will spark innovation. New inventors will not be required to ask financing of an overbearing capital venture firm or banks. Instead an eager college graduate can look to friends to create something together by pooling their "national inheritance." Big corporations often don't innovate; they suppress competition and innovation once grown. They buyout small innovative companies similar to how Facebook bought out WhatsApp and Instagram.

Trusting the average person by giving them land and education is what created America. In contrast, entrusting our country to corporations or governments is what's tearing it down. It may seem that such a system would be too dangerous, for then the many, not the few, would control the country but that is exactly what is needed and that is democracy. Only the masses must be well educated and informed. It was very dangerous for Toyota to give its employees full control over stopping the factory's production line (costing thousands of dollars with each stop), something the American car manufacturers would not dare attempt. Yet once the power to control was given to the average worker, instead of abusing their new found power, such a vote of confidence did exactly the opposite, it gave the workers a renewed sense of unity and pride in their work resulting in phenomenal growth. Such trust in their employees also made Toyota the greatest car manufacturer in modern times. Trust allowed them to take over a failed General Motors factory and with essentially the same workforce turned it into the most productive car manufacturing plant in America.

Instead of creating a system in which greed and manipulation of others is the only way to get ahead, we need to create a system in which cooperation and honesty are the ways to get ahead. If someone uses unsavory ways to become rich, they will quickly lose support and their children will be unable to continue their abusive ways. On the other hand, if someone is the useful-rich, the next generation will still become rich since they are actually useful. Furthermore, they will be helped to climb the hierarchy once again for they are useful.

Starting with self-love (namely greed) will only worsen the situation. It's a wonder we are beginning to see the results now. America has been teaching greed to the generations that follow for decades and it will take monumental effort to turn this tide of selfishness around. This exaltation of selfishness is now looming over our country and the whole world. We need to build a system that starts with others: love your neighbor before you love yourself. We need an alternative to lying to the next generation and instructing them, "do the best for you and it will be the best for others." It's time to create a system that says "do the best for others and it will be what's good for you." When the majority start at the same level we can actually have a global system, then we can actually use the enormous untapped potential of humanity to have a better world not by wasting the majority of our potential on weapons or the stock market, but by turning our eyes away from the self and onto our neighbor, onto millions in America and billions around the world that need America to be that shining city on a hill.

Afterword

I always thought my father was odd for insisting that America won World War II because they were a Christian country. Now, I believe him wholeheartedly, because unity, fairness, and freedom have unquantifiable benefits that unfortunately America has largely lost. Morality and technological advancement need to be balanced and when they are not, we will always get conflict. It is my sincere hope that we can end conflict, yet the reality is the more we turn our societies into a dog-eat-dog jungle the more conflict will increase nationally and internationally.

A massive gulf exists between Jesus' teaching and anything we do nowadays. Unfortunately, we have followed the "Gospel of Greed" hook, line, and sinker, but it's not too late. Once we decide that feudalism and slavery are just as wrong as inherited capital, then we can move forward. Only then, can we step closer to "love thy neighbor as thyself," and only then can we reap the rewards of performing the correct action.

Having read this far, my job is almost done and your job is just starting. I did my best to clarify where we are headed, you can decide to ignore my warning of what's to come and continue on this self-destructive path and bring the whole world to the edge again and again, or you can decide to change course, If you wait because it's too hard and it will require too much sacrifice, understand that the longer you wait the harder it will be to right this ship and the next time we reap what we sow, it might be our last. Just as the frog will not leave the pot even as it's being slowly cooked to death, greed and pride are slowly destroying us and we refuse to see it. We can choose to take serious steps to stop this slow approaching annihilation of humanity or decide we like the warm water until it's too late.

Doing the right thing is always harder than doing the wrong thing or doing nothing. Ending monarchy was an immense struggle and cost dearly. Liberating the slaves pitted brother against brother, yet the cost can't be compared to the rewards and progress achieved afterward. In this case, living by the next self-evident truth will reap us two rewards: avert another impending disaster and help take us to the next level of equality and its consequently associated cohesion and harmony.

Just as I started the book by describing the wrong lessons I have learned; I will end it with some correct lessons. I don't know where we are going; I just know that we are heading the wrong way and it's time we made a U-turn as soon as possible.

Far from not having free will, free will is all we are. With our will we can choose to be moral and live up to our ideals or decide to be amoral and ignore our self-evident truth. With our will, we can choose life or we can choose death. There are an infinite number of ways to choose death and only one way to choose life and the only way to choose life is always going to be "love your neighbor as yourself." In all the social sciences the closer we get to "love thy neighbor as yourself," the better off we will be.

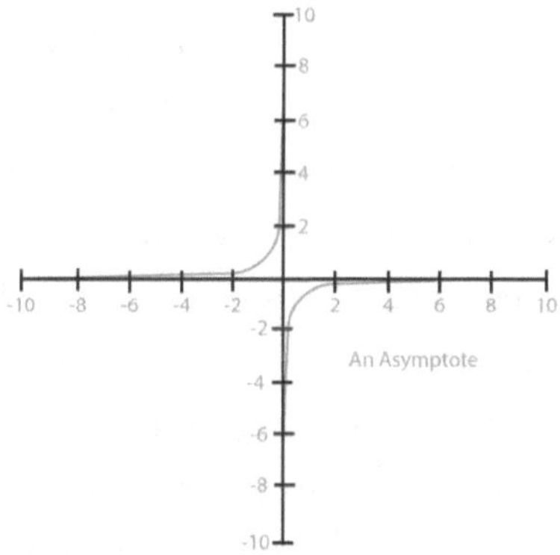

Figure 8

Just like the asymptote in y=-0.5/x (Figure 8) that will forever chase the ideal, we will forever try to understand and perfect what it means to "love your neighbor as yourself." Let's stop looking back at what we used to be. Let's stop trying to learn from what we used to do. We will never do anything new looking further and further in the past. We don't look at how apes live and try to imitate their behaviors. We don't look at how they solve problems to model ourselves after them, so why do we always try to be animals in the way we treat each other? Are we improving or digressing? Are we becoming more moral, or will we always find excuses to harm each other in the name of pride? Is it time to grow up yet? It's curious and telling that we love to point at chimpanzees and use them for our morality only when it's convenient.

Only when it comes to sexuality, do some feel it necessary to invoke chimps' behavior, but when it comes to eating their young, with such behaviour our desire for imitation cease's; it seems we can control ourselves after all!! Loving your neighbor as yourself is the unifying theory of all the social sciences. If you want to improve, then make that your target. When we stray far from it, we will "reap what we sow." When we come closer to it, "we will reap what we sow." Let's choose to love our neighbor as ourselves and let's stop being "blind to the obvious, and blind to our blindness" (Kahneman). Maybe soon we can sing with John Newton that old slave ship captain turned pastor who was instrumental in ending slavery: "Amazing grace, how sweet the sound, that saved a wretch like me, I once was lost, but now am found, was blind but now I see."

Choosing life is choosing to love your neighbor as yourself. Choosing life is to not see any difference between you and the other seven billion people living on this planet. Choosing life is deciding there is no me versus them, not even us versus others, but only "we" and realizing if we don't elect "we," then we choose death.

Humanity has spent far too long thinking, me versus them. We imagined ourselves civilized ever since we turned me versus them into us versus them. In truth, "us versus them" is far more dangerous and potentially destructive and will end all of us, if we keep pushing that narrative. We will not affect genuine and lasting change until we choose life, until we adopt an all of us worldview, the selfish gene will not adopt an others worldview. We must show the world an example of how it should be done not by just admonishing others or worse by using force to turn them democratic. We need to show that if we who are from every corner of the world can be one cohesive country, they can manage it as well. From the days of Moses, man has always had a choice. With that choice comes consequences. Let's stop listening to the voice urging us to harm others to get ahead and know harming others is harming ourselves and future generations.

> *For this commandment which I command thee this day, it is not hidden from thee, neither is it far off. It is not in heaven, that thou shouldest say, who shall go up for us to heaven, and bring it unto us, that we may hear it, and do it? Neither is it beyond the sea, that thou shouldest say, who shall go over the sea for us, and bring it unto us, that we may hear it, and do it? But the word is very nigh unto thee, in thy mouth, and in thy heart, that thou mayest do it See, I have set before thee this day life and good, and death and evil;*
>
> Deu 30:11-15 (KJV)

Our fate has always been in our hands. We might not recognize how we are shaping our own destiny, but every decision, large or small, is shaping who we are and shaping the world we will eventually inherit. It's time for a new race of humans, who run a new kind of Race.

Bibliography

de Waal, F. (2016). *Primates and Philosophers: How Morality Evolved.* Princeton University Press; Princeton

Carlson, B. (2013) Tesla: Inventor of the Electrical Age. University Press; Princeton

Cavenaugh, K. (2018). "How much is enough?" Ted Lecture. Available from: www.ted.com/talks/kevin_cavenaugh_how_much_is_enough

Chang H. (2009). *Bad Samaritans: The Myth of Free Trade and the Secret History of Capitalism.* Bloomsbury; London

Chesterton, G. K. (1908; 2008) *Orthodoxy*. Waking Lion Press; West Valley City

Harari, Y. (2017). *Homo Deus: A History of Tomorrow*. Harvill Sacker; London

Kahneman, D. (2012). *Thinking, Fast and Slow*. Farrar, Straus, & Giroux; New York

Lafrance, Adrienne "Disasters That Were Foretold."

Available from: *https://www.theatlantic.com*, https://www.theatlantic.com/national/archive/2015/09/hurricane-katrina-and-other-preventable-disasters/401123/.

Lewis, C. S. (1952). *Mere Christianity.* Geoffrey Bles; London

Milanovic, B (2016). *Global Inequality.* Harvard University Press, Cambridge, MA

Murray, C. (2012). *Coming Apart: The State of White America, 1960–2010.* Crown Publishing Group; New York

Peterson, J. (2017).'Jordan Peterson on the evolutionary origin of values'. Available from: https://www.youtube.com/watch?v=mFTjPZ7NSPE

Pickett, K. & R. Wilkinson (2009). *Spirit level.* Allen Lane; London

Piff, P. (2013). "Does money make you mean?" Ted Talk. Available from: www.ted.com/talks/paul_piff_-does_money_make_you_mean

Reich, R. (2020). *The System: Who Rigged It, How We Fix It.* Pan Macmillan; London

Tikkanen, Roosa, & Melinda K. K. Abrams, "U.S. Health Care from a Global Perspective, 2019: Higher Spending, Worse Outcomes?" *The Commonwealth Fund*, 2020. Available from: https://www.commonwealthfund.org/publications/issue-briefs/2020/jan/us-health-care-global-perspective-2019

Wilson T. (2002) *Strangers to Ourselves: Discovering the Adaptive Unconscious.* Harvard University Press; Cambridge MA

Wolff, Richard, talks on Google. Available from:

https://www.commonwealthfund.org/publications/issue-briefs/2020/jan/us-health-care-global-perspective-2019

Piketty, T. (2017). *Capital in the Twenty-First Century.* Harvard University Press, Cambridge, MA

Acknowledgments

In a real sense each and every person I argued with deserves to have their name here, since I always argue, this section would be extremely long. I like start by thanking my editor Rebecca Collins who took a book full of errors and turned it into something readable, also her son Josh Collins who helped all the illustrations in the book. Also, I would like to thank the very talented Divya Balu for creating the book cover. Also, I'd like to thank my critics/contributors: Ben Walker, Rob Jackson, Miks Kalnins, and Dr. Bob Scales. Finally, I want to extend a special thank you for Shirly Wang who listened to me ramble on many times as I asked her many hard questions. Shirly's friendship and dialogue helped lay the foundation for this book.

Made in United States
Troutdale, OR
11/03/2026

56847370R00111